Contents

1. Researching school exclusion   **1**

2. Education: the legacy of the New Right and
  New Labour   **10**

3. The perceptions of excluded pupils   **21**

4. The perceptions of parents/carers   **34**

5. The perceptions of teachers   **49**

6. The perceptions of support workers   **78**

7. Findings and policy implications   **115**

8. Understanding secondary school exclusion:
  the production of docile bodies   **120**

Acknowledgements

In order to protect the confidentiality of the respondents it is, unfortunately, not possible to mention names. Suffice to say, many thanks to all the young people, parents/carers, teachers and support workers who gave up their time to talk to us. Thanks also to those at the Behaviour Support Service who both inspired this research and helped to facilitate the interviews. Finally, thanks to the Nuffield Foundation for providing funding support. This book is dedicated to 'Glen', 'William', 'Jack', 'Cheryl', 'Dave', 'Jeremy', 'Joanna' and 'Nancy', who all resisted complying with a repressive system.

Chapter one

Researching school exclusion

Background

Education is central to inclusion, offering a route into social, political and economic involvement. Low levels of participation in school, therefore, have profound implications for a child's future. Yet still, significant numbers of children are marginalised from mainstream education provision in Britain because they are perceived as having 'behavioural problems'. Between 1990/91 and 1998/99, the number of recorded permanent exclusions rose from 2,910 to 10,400 (Hayden and Dunne, 2001), while many others are temporarily or 'unofficially' excluded (Osler *et al.*, 2001). This trend is damaging to both society and the life chances of children (Blyth and Milner, 1993), making it a crucial issue for government (Ahier *et al.*, 1996).

Media reporting on the problem of school exclusion can be dramatic. For example, on 27 July 2000, *Guardian Education* carried a report under the headline *'Fear Rules'* describing *'alarming levels of violence against teachers'* in Birmingham secondary schools (p.2). Again, on 21 September 2001, *The Guardian* claimed that *'children as young as three are making teachers' lives hell'* (p.17). The report described a 'rising tide' of physical and verbal aggression between pupils and directed at teachers in nursery, primary and secondary schools. In contrast, however, some argue that *'behaviour in schools is largely very good'* with most schools *'havens of peace in the turbulent lives of their pupils'* (Dunford, 2001: 20).

The reasons offered for school exclusion conflict. Some, including the former Secretary of State for Education, David Blunkett, blame poor parenting and the breakdown of societal discipline (*The Guardian*, 28 April and 13 July 2000). Others stress structural factors including poverty, culture and social policies (Cohen *et al.*, 1994). A UNICEF report published in June 2000 suggests Britain has one of the worst records on child poverty in the industrialised world, with around 20 per cent of young people living in families with incomes below half median earnings (*The Observer*, 11 June 2000). The cost of poverty to children is inadequate nutrition, housing and health, factors that impinge not only on their intellectual development (Ahmed, 2000) but also life expectancy (*The Independent*, 19 October 2000). While the disproportionate number of African-Caribbean children excluded suggests a correlation with ethnicity (CRE, 1997, SEU, 1998, Craig *et al.*, 1998, Cohen *et al.*, 1994), studies suggest that social class is the most significant factor influencing the educational experience

(Parelius and Parelius, 1987). The organisational culture of schools and the lower expectations some teachers have of working-class pupils in terms of achievement and behaviour appear to exacerbate the problem by intensifying psychological problems for these pupils (Coleman, 1998). There is also evidence to suggest that selection processes in schools *'competing in the market place for the most "rewarding" pupils'* (Lloyd-Smith and Davies, 1995: 6) are exacerbating the influences of class, ethnicity and poverty (Beynon and Glavanis, 1999, Cohen 1994a and 1994b, Coleman, 1998, Taylor *et al.,* 1997). Additionally, the rigid results-oriented regime imposed on schools appears to be placing extra burdens on pupils already experiencing difficulties with conventional curriculum-based work:

> *'Ever since the national curriculum was introduced, schools have been forced to be more prescriptive ... So they are less able to meet the needs of some children ... The more recent framework of league tables and inspection makes it even harder for them to cater for difficult or disturbed pupils'.* (Jane Oliver, education services manager for Bernardo's Knotley project, Croydon, cited in George, 2001: 131)

In 1999 the Office for National Statistics (ONS) reported that 10 per cent of Britain's children suffer a mental disorder (anxiety, depression, behaviour disorders and/or hyperactivity), and that this was concentrated among children of poor households. In families where both parents are unemployed, 20 per cent of children have a mental health problem. Children with a mental illness were four times more likely to truant, three times more likely to have specific learning difficulties and ten times more likely to be in trouble with the police (ONS, 1999, cited in Davies, 2000: 6). These are all problems linked to types of behaviour that lead to children being excluded from school (Davies, 2000).

Not only does the current education system appear to place additional burdens on pupils, it also appears to be a significant cause of a teacher shortage that, in turn, exacerbates 'difficult' behaviour. Caroline Wigmore, chair of the Professional Association of Teachers, argues that the present system *'treats staff like robots and pupils like products on a conveyor belt'*, adding that teaching staff live in fear of being judged incompetent. This, she states, leads teachers to put further pressure on their pupils, adding to their difficulties. Moreover, she claims it is driving many teachers away from the profession, particularly because of the constant *'soul destroying form filling'* needed to satisfy inspectors (cited in Smithers, 2000: 7). In turn, staff shortages are seen by OFSTED as having an adverse impact on pupil behaviour, demotivated by the increased use of ill-qualified, inexperienced and temporary teachers (Woodward, 2001).

Only about one third of excluded children are quickly reintegrated back into school. The remainder often receive what is known as 'education otherwise', arranged in most cases through special centres (SEU, 1998). Marginalising pupils into off-site educational provision can reinforce the message that they are unacceptable. In recognition of this, there has been an increasing lobby for inclusive education (Lloyd-Smith and Davies, 1995). The Social Exclusion Unit (SEU) report on truancy and school exclusion presented to Parliament in 1998, proposed a number of measures that would seek to reduce by one third the number of permanent and fixed-term exclusions by 2002, while providing alternative full-time appropriate education for all pupils excluded for more than three weeks (SEU, 1998). This report was followed by Circular 10/99, setting out guidance on the current law and good practice on pupil exclusion and reintegration (DfEE, 1999a), and Circular 11/99, setting out further guidance on the administrative and legal responsibilities of Local Education Authorities (LEAs) for educating and reintegrating excluded pupils (DfEE, 1999b). Revisions to government guidance were made in 2000 and 2001 while, at the time of writing, further revisions were being proposed through a consultation exercise (DfES, 2002). The report *Opportunity for All: Tackling poverty and social exclusion* (DSS, 1999) restated the government's commitment to reducing school exclusions. Further guidance on diagnosing 'inclusive schools' is contained in *Evaluating Educational Inclusion* (OFSTED, undated). Within current guidance, there is little evidence that the structural causes of school exclusion have been acknowledged - not surprising given that New Labour ministers have denied that these considerations are relevant. For instance, David Blunkett decried as *'cynics'* those who claim educational performance is related to socio-economic influences (Carvel 2000: 11).

Research aims

This research aims to build on existing studies by exploring the nature of school exclusion from the perspective of excluded pupils themselves. Central to its approach is the notion that children should be empowered to participate actively in the research process:

> '*A consensus has developed around the belief that the ethics, tools and roles employed in qualitative children's research should empower children. Empowerment is associated with allowing children to choose to become active participants in the research process, employing tools which offer children the maximum opportunity to put forward their views and reducing the social distance and re-negotiating the power relations between researcher and child.*' (Davis, 1998: 329)

Consequently, this study reflects the spirit of the 1989 Children Act which requires young people to be offered the opportunity to participate in decision-making processes affecting their lives. It also reflects Article 12 of the UN Convention on the Rights of the Child, ratified by the British government in 1991, supporting the rights of children to participate in society. In respect of school exclusion, the meaningful participation of excluded pupils can have a crucial role to play in their successful reintegration. As Thomas and O'Kane argue:

> *'Rather than reinforce views of children's incompetence by portraying them as victims, we have to develop methods that allow us to explore children's capacities, needs and interests from their own point of view.'*
> (Thomas and O'Kane, 1998: 346)

While the government, however, is committed to involving children in the design and delivery of its policies on social exclusion (DSS, 1999), children's involvement in schools remains a minority activity, especially for pupils with special educational needs (Lloyd-Smith and Davies, 1995). Moreover, there have been:

> *'few sociological studies based on children's accounts of their everyday lives and experiences, and sociologists and anthropologists are increasingly aware that there are large gaps in our understanding of children's perspectives ... This general lack of basic social research means it is difficult to incorporate children's perspectives in policy terms.'*
> (Morrow, 1999: 297-298)

This research, therefore, aims to add to our understanding of school exclusion by exploring the 'lived realities' of excluded pupils themselves through a sociological analysis of their perceptions. In this respect it takes a similar approach to recent work by Hayden and Dunne (2001). They suggest that inclusive policies need to be built on a better understanding of the experiences of excluded pupils and their parents, and that this requires giving families a greater voice in the debate about inclusion. Their research found that pupils and their parents shared a deep sense of injustice following their experience of exclusion, and that the reasons given for expulsion were often disproportionate or unsubstantiated. There was also a sense that children's specific needs (such as learning difficulties) had not been met due to the unavailability of adequate resources. Parents also felt that both they and their children had received insufficient support before and after exclusion, while children had been left on average four months out of school before any formal educational provision was received. Proposals suggested by Hayden and Dunne include earlier intervention with parental involvement to prevent exclusions, the availability of trained staff to provide appropriate support, and greater involvement of pupils and parents (supported by independent advocacy) in the exclusion process (Hayden and Dunne, 2001).

Methodology

With financial support from the Nuffield Foundation, this research was conducted in a major British city experiencing significant rises in the number of pupils excluded from school. The city was chosen because the local education authority's Behaviour Support Service (BSS) fully supported independent research and offered full co-operation. The research focused on a pilot study of eight pupils aged 11 to 16, all excluded from mainstream education. The sample was not representative as the pilot was partly to test whether the proposed research technique was useful when working with pupils with 'difficult behaviour'. Although we believe our approach has produced rich and deep insights into exclusionary processes in the education system, we would recommend a fuller study to gain a more representative response. The research examined qualitative issues raised in focus-group meetings held with four of the eight pupils. The issues raised informed the design of a schedule of questions used to explore in greater depth the perceptions not only of the eight pupils and their parents/carers, but also teachers and behaviour support workers. This allowed us to consider the complex interplay between school factors and pupils' behaviour, thereby permitting a broader understanding to that offered by Hayden and Dunne.

The focus-group meetings with the children were arranged with the help of one of the City's Behaviour Support Centres (BSCs). The centre identified eight pupils who, with their parents'/carers' consent, agreed in principle to participate in the research. A leaflet entitled *School Exclusion: What do you think?* was prepared and sent with a covering letter to each pupil and their parent(s)/carer(s), thanking them for agreeing to help with the project and explaining more about it: who we were; how we planned to carry out the project; what would happen to the information collected; and the confidential nature of the findings. It was originally planned to hold four weekly sessions at the BSC covering four themes: schools and teachers; home and family; friends and community; and future aspirations. The first meeting with the eight pupils was arranged for a day in May 2000. Refreshments were provided. Only four pupils attended. The meeting started with personal introductions followed by an introductory talk explaining the aims of the research, why it was important, how it would be conducted and the ethical issues involved (i.e. it was not a test and would be non-judgmental; anything said would be treated in confidence; and that if the pupils felt uncomfortable at any time they could withdraw). Group discussions, brainstorming sessions and a two-page questionnaire were then used to explore the children's experiences of schools and teachers. At the end of the two-hour session it was agreed that all four pupils would return to the centre the following week. We felt, however, that they may not wish to proceed with four full sessions so we incorporated the remaining three themes - home and family, friends and community, and future aspirations - into one final session. All four pupils returned for the second week. Brainstorming and a proforma addressing the remaining themes were used in the final session. At the end of this, and after negotiation with the pupils, it was decided not to proceed with further sessions. Additional information was gathered via an in-school support worker based in one of the City's inner-city schools. This included written work and drawings produced by pupils identified as having 'behavioural problems'.

Following the focus-group meetings and an examination of the additional information gathered, schedules of questions were designed around the concerns and issues raised by the pupils. These would be used in one-to-one structured interviews with the same four pupils plus four others identified by the BSS, making eight in total[1], together with their parents/carers. The schedule of questions covered aspects of the pupils' and parents'/carers' experience of:

- school exclusion;
- schools and teachers; and
- local neighbourhood, 'home', community, friends and future aspirations.

Letters were sent to the parents/carers explaining the purpose of the interviews and the way they would be conducted. Following their consent, taped interviews were carried out with pupils and their parents/carers in June, July and August 2000. Following these, arrangements were made to interview eight teachers and eight support workers. Initial approaches were made by telephone and letter to head teachers in inner-city schools identified in the City Council's directory *Secondary Education Opportunities for your child*. 15 schools were contacted before eight teachers willing to be interviewed were identified. Generally,

---

[1] **Pupil respondents and their parent(s)/carer(s) – names have been changed to protect the respondents' confidentiality:**

- Glen, age 16, White British, living with his mother, Grace, and step-father. Live in a housing association property in a deprived inner-city area. Step-father works as a lorry-driver earning in excess of £201 per week.
- William, age 14, African-Caribbean, living with his mother, Winnie, and his brother and sister. Live in a council house in a deprived inner-city area. Both William and his mother have sickle-cell anaemia. The family live on benefits.
- Jack, White British, age 13, living with his mother, Jenny, and his two brothers. Live in a council house on an inner-city estate. The family live on benefits.
- Cheryl, African-Caribbean, age 14, living with her mother, Carol, and three brothers and sister. Live in a council house on a peripheral estate. The family live on benefits.
- Dave, White British, age 13, living with his carer, Dawn, since May 2, 2000. Live in a council house on a peripheral estate. The family live on benefits.
- Jeremy, White British, age 13, living with his mother, Joan, and two sisters. Live in a housing association house in the inner-city. Mother is a dinner-lady earning between £100-£150 per week.
- Joanna, White British, age 13, living with her father, Jim, mother, brother and step-daughter. Live in an owner-occupied house in a City suburb. Jim earns in excess of £200 per week
- Nancy, White British, age 14, living with her mother, Nina, and sister in a council house on a peripheral estate. Nina works as a barperson earning between £51-£100 per week.

teachers seemed less available or willing to be interviewed than pupils and their parents/carers. Eight willing support workers were identified with the assistance of another in-school support worker. Taped interviews were conducted with teachers and support workers between September 2000 and February 2001. Interviews with teachers covered themes connected with managing discipline in school, and teachers and schooling. Interviews with support workers covered themes connected with supporting excluded pupils, and teachers and schooling. The transcription of the taped interviews was completed by May 2001.

The analysis of the data gathered is conducted in two parts. The first, in Chapter 7, compares perceptions of the four respondent groups. Common concerns with implications for social policy are identified. The second part of the analysis, in Chapter 8, locates school exclusion within a sociological context, offering a conceptually rich insight into exclusionary processes within the education system itself. Chapters 3 to 6 set out the perceptions of the four respondent groups in detail. Extensive quotes are presented, contrasting significantly to much of the existing literature into school exclusion which tends to privilege the voice of the researcher over that of the researched. At the end of each of these four chapters key issues raised are summarised. Before examining and analysing these perceptions, Chapter 2 sets out the broader policy context within which school exclusion in the UK is practised.

Summary findings

The main findings of this study are:

- Pupils who challenge education practices are being victimised by their disciplinary regime.

- Teachers are being de-professionalised and losing control over teaching practice.

- The marketisation of education has resulted in the erosion of its social objectives.

- A marketised education system works against notions of 'citizenship' (social opportunity and democracy) and social inclusion.

- There is an urgent need to rethink the function of education, particularly in relation to humanistic values.

References

Ahier, J., Cosin, B. and Hales, M. (eds) (1996) *Diversity and Change: Education, Policy and Selection*, London: Routledge.

Ahmed, K. (2000) 'Britain shamed by child poverty', *The Observer*, 11 June, p.1.

Beynon, H. and Glavanis, P. (eds) (1999) *Patterns of Social Inequality*, London: Longman.

Blyth, E. and Milner, J. (1993) 'Exclusion from School: A First Step in Exclusion from Society?', *Children & Society*, 7:3, pp. 255-268.

Carvel, J. (2000) 'Poverty no excuse for failure, says Blunkett', *The Guardian*, 2 March, p.11.

Cohen, R. (1994a) *Exclusion from School: The Family Perspective*, paper to National Children's Bureau Conference, 11 October.

Cohen, R. (1994b) 'Outside Looking In', *Community Care*, 15-21 Dec., pp.24-25.

Cohen, R. and Hughes, M. with Ashworth, L. and Blair, M. (1994) *School's Out: The Family Perspective on School Exclusion*, London: Barnardo's/FSU.

Coleman, J.W. (1998) *Social Problems: A Brief Introduction*, London: Longman.

Commission for Racial Equality (CRE) (1997) *Exclusion from School and Racial Equality: A Good Practice Guide*, London: CRE.

Craig, G., Elliott-White, M. and Perkins, N. (1998), *Mapping Disaffected Youth*, Papers in Social Research No 10, Lincoln: University of Lincolnshire & Humberside.

Davies, N. (2000) 'The tower block children for whom school has no point', *The Guardian*, 10 July, p.1 and pp.6-7.

Davis, J.M. (1998) 'Understanding The Meanings of Children: A Reflexive Process', *Children & Society*, 12:5, November, pp.325-335.

(DfEE) Department for Education and Employment (1999a) *Social Inclusion: Pupil Support*, Circular 10/99, London: DfEE.

(DfEE) Department for Education and Employment (1999b) *Social Inclusion: the LEA role in Pupil Support*, Circular 11/99, London: DfEE.

(DfEE) Department for Education and Employment (2002) *Revised Guidance on Exclusion from School: Draft for Consultation*, London: DfEE.

(DSS) Department of Social Security (1999) *Opportunity for All: Tackling poverty and social exclusion*, London: The Stationary Office.

Dunford, J. (2001) 'Making pupils behave', *The Guardian*, 12 February, p.20.

George, M. (2001) 'A way back to the fold', *Guardian Society*, 19 Sept, p.131.

Hayden, C. and Dunne, S. (2001) *Outside, looking in: Children's and families' experiences of exclusion from school*, London: The Children's Society.

Lloyd-Smith, M. and Davies J.W. (1995) *On the Margins: The Educational Experience of 'Problem' Pupils*, Stoke-on-Trent: Trentham Books.

Morrow, V. (1999) 'If you were a teacher, it would be harder to talk to you: reflections on qualitative research with children in school', *International Journal of Social Research Methodology*, 1:4, pp.297-313.

OFSTED (undated) *Evaluating Educational Inclusion: Guidance for inspectors and schools*, Inspection Quality Division, London: OFSTED.

Osler, A., Watling, R., Busher, H., Cole, T. and White, A. (2001) *Reasons for Exclusion from School*, Research Brief No.244, London: DfEE.

Parelius, P.J. and Parelius, A.P. (1987) *The Sociology of Education*, 2nd Edition, Englewood Cliffs, NJ: Prentice-Hall.

Smithers, R. (2000) 'Fear 'forcing teachers to quit'', *The Guardian*, 2 Aug, p.7.

(SEU) Social Exclusion Unit (1998) *Truancy and School Exclusion Report by the Social Exclusion Unit*, London: The Cabinet Office.

Taylor, S., Rizvi, F., Lingard, B. and Henry, M. (1997) *Educational Policy and the Politics of Change*, London: Routledge.

Thomas, N. and O'Kane, C. (1998) 'The Ethics of Participatory Research with Children', *Children & Society*, 12:5, November, pp.336-348.

Woodward, W. (2001) 'Worsening behaviour 'linked to teacher shortage'', *The Guardian*, 7 February, p.6.

Chapter two

Education: the legacy of the New Right and New Labour

Background

This chapter sets out the contemporary policy context within which school exclusion in Britain is practised. It begins by examining the changing context of state education in British before then considering the effects of the radical reforms of the 1980s and 1990s. It concludes with an assessment of New Labour policies during its four years of government after 1997. This assessment demonstrates that New Labour in government accepted most of the previous Conservative education reforms. As a consequence, it is suggested that exclusionary processes within the education system are likely to continue.

The changing context of state education in Britain

The post-war welfare state was largely organised on the basis of bureaucratic administration (established sets of rules and regulations that generally sought to ensure conformity and impartiality in the delivery of services) and professionalism (allowing some degree of expert judgement, especially in the National Health Service) (Clarke and Newman, 1997). By the 1960s, this system of organising social welfare came under attack from both sides of the political spectrum. Despite the idea of bureaucratic neutrality, evidence pointed to persistent inequalities in all areas of welfare, leading to calls from the political left for more democratic and collective forms of provision. At the same time, welfare bureaucrats came under attack from the Conservative Right for having vested interests and making extravagant demands. It was this latter critique – an attack on the monopoly status of state welfare institutions - that came to dominate the political landscape after 1979.

The origins of state intervention in education can be situated around 1833 when public funds were first advanced to finance largely church schooling, although some state-provided education also existed in workhouses, prisons and the armed forces. In 1862 a system of inspections for subsidised schools was introduced, and academic performance and school attendance would influence the funding made available (Burden *et al.*, 2000). The (Forster) Elementary Education Act 1870 established School Boards, elected authorities charged with setting up and funding (from the rates) schools where existing provision was deficient. Attendance was not compulsory until 1880, initially to the age of 10 years. This was extended to 11 years in 1893 and to 12 years in 1899 (Trowler, 1998). This early intervention was largely aimed at ensuring adequate schooling for working-class children, to habituate them to obedience and provide them with the basic literacy and numeracy skills required for capitalist wage labour (Burden et al., 2000). The middle and upper classes would send their children (usually males) to independent or public schools where they would study a curriculum that included the classics and high culture (Trowler, 1998, Burden et al., 2000). A shift in emphasis in education policy occurred in the early twentieth century under the influence of the new Liberals. This tradition aspired to promote equality of opportunity through education by exposing the working class to a curriculum adapted from that in public schools. The (Balfour) Education Act 1902 made local education authorities (LEAs) rather than School Boards responsible for schools. The Act also made provision for some working-class access to secondary education. In 1907, 25 per cent of places in secondary schools were to be free. The 1918 Education Act raised the school-leaving age to 14 years (Trowler, 1998).

The Second World War had a major impact on British education. In particular, the radicalism fostered by the war led to renewed support for education as a civil right (Burden et al., 2000). The 1943 Norwood Report put forward proposals for the tripartite system that emerged after the war under the Education Act 1944 - the grammar, secondary modern and technical schools (Trowler, 1998). The 1944 Act established compulsory free state education for 5 to 15-year-olds. While the Act aimed to achieve a meritocratic education system, research showed the 11-plus examination to be biased towards middle-class children. For instance, the 1954 Gurney-Dixon Report, Early Leaving, concluded that a pupil's educational performance was closely linked to the social class of their parents (Trowler, 1998). Later, the 1967 Plowden Report led to experimental projects in positive discrimination through the designation of Educational Priority Areas (EPAs) aimed at improving schooling in deprived inner-city areas. EPAs had little effect, however, on the relationship between educational attainment and class (Burden et al., 2000). In 1965 Harold Wilson's Labour government introduced plans to reorganize the tripartite school system into a comprehensive one, where non-selective schools would simply accept any child from their catchment area, consolidating a trend that had started in the 1950s. By 1982 around 80 per cent of secondary-school pupils were attending comprehensives (Trowler, 1998).

In 1976 economic crisis and the intervention of the International Monetary Fund (IMF) led to major changes in British social policy. Over the period 1975-79 the proportion of gross domestic product (GDP) spent on education fell from 7 per cent to 5.8 per cent. The Labour government of the time broke with the traditional social democratic perspective on equality in education, bringing to the fore issues around curriculum development, educational standards, teacher competence and the vocational relevance of schooling (Burden et al., 2000). Prime Minister James Callaghan's 1976 Ruskin speech, attacking the education system for the economic failings of the time, marked something of a watershed in education policy:

> '*I am concerned in my journeys to find complaints from industry that new recruits from schools sometimes do not have the basic tools to do the job that is required ... The goals of our education ... are clear enough. They are to equip children to the best of their ability for a lively, constructive place in society and also to fit them to do a job of work [and] to be basically literate, to be basically numerate, to understand how to live and work together, to have respect for others and respect for the individual.*'
> (Cited in Trowler, 1998: 4)

Callaghan was concerned about the curriculum taught in schools, which he felt had little to do with work skills. His ideas effectively paved the way for the advancement of a new direction in British education policy under the Conservative New Right.

Education policy and the New Right

The Conservative government elected in 1979 continued with policies initiated by Labour aimed at emphasising the occupational function of education and raising standards. Burden *et al.* (2000) identify four key areas of reform in the education system during the Conservatives' years in office from 1979 to 1997: first, a reduced role for local authorities; second, an attack on professionalism; third, the expansion of 'quasi-markets'; and fourth, the elevation of the role and power of management. The role of local authorities was reduced through Local Management of Schools (LMS) and opting out. The attack on professionalism came from increasing the power of governing bodies, the imposition of the national curriculum, and Office for Standards in Education (OFSTED) directives on what and how to teach. In addition, salaries of teachers fell relative to other white-collar incomes. The expansion of the market came in the form of competition between schools for student numbers and the imposition of business values. Lastly, the power of management was advanced through heads adopting business practices based on the private sector. Underpinning these reforms was the New Right belief that bureaucratic procedures hindered the effectiveness of service delivery (Clarke *et al.*, 2000). Consequently, the 'old ways' of managing public services came under attack:

> '*Bureaucrats were identified as actively hostile to the public - hiding behind the impersonality of regulations and 'red tape' to deny choice, building bureaucratic empires at the expense of providing service, and insulated from the "real world" pressures of competition by their monopolistic position. Professionals were arraigned as motivated by self-interest, exercising power over would be consumers, denying choice through the dubious claim that "professionals know best"*'.
> (Clarke and Newman, 1997: 15)

State institutions were to experience privatisation and the imposition of the market discipline, opening up welfare provision to competition and new forms of control. These changes were justified in the name of economic efficiency and extending consumer choice (such as tenants' rights to buy their council house or parents' rights to choose what school their child attends). They were also intended to change the public's perception of the meaning of 'welfare', and to discourage 'welfare dependency' and encourage individuals to take more responsibility for themselves.

The Education Act 1980 required LEAs (local education authorities) to allow parental choice in determining the school their child would attend, as well as parent representation on school governing bodies. More fundamental reforms to the education system came with the Education Reform Act 1988, which introduced LMS - allowing schools to be run by governing bodies similar to boards of directors in the private sector. School income would depend on the number of pupils recruited, with 'good' schools (based on academic standards and position in league tables) expected to gain and expand while 'poor' schools would get less money and contract. Competition would be further encouraged by allowing schools to opt out of LEA control and become 'grant maintained' (GMS), receiving their funds directly from the government.

The 1988 Act also contained plans for a national curriculum. A National Curriculum Council was established to control what would be taught in schools. Three core compulsory subjects were specified - English, Mathematics and Science – and seven compulsory foundation subjects - History, Geography, Technology, Art, Music, Physical Education and, for those 11 to 16-years-of-age, a modern language. Religious education had to be provided for pupils whose parents wished it. Three cross-curricula subjects - Health Education, Personal and Social Education, and Careers - had to be taught through other subjects (Burden *et al.*, 2000). The national curriculum was designed to take up around 80 per cent of school time, so other subjects had to be fitted into the remaining 20 per cent of time. The system is highly prescriptive, with detailed handbooks specifying what has to be taught at each stage in each subject.

Another major innovation in 1992 was the replacement of Her Majesty's Inspectorate for schools with OFSTED. It became instantly clear that OFSTED saw itself as establishing a role in rooting out 'inadequate teaching' and 'failing schools'. It subsequently expanded its role to promoting 'effective' teaching methods. Moreover, OFSTED sought to provide evidence consistent with New Right ideology that social background did not account for the 'poor' educational attainment found in schools in deprived areas. It also claimed that class size did not significantly affect educational attainment. The implication of these arguments is that uniformly high levels of educational attainment could be achieved regardless of the social conditions in which pupils lived, so long as good teachers deploying teaching methods prescribed by OFSTED were employed (Burden *et al.*, 2000). Implicit here is the notion that inequalities will be reduced if education standards are raised. Altogether, then, these reforms reflect the Conservatives' belief that:

> '*By encouraging schools to compete for pupils, introducing new funding arrangements, providing opportunities for open enrolment, opting out, requiring the publication of league tables and establishing new forms of inspection, schools ... will become more effective, efficient and generally improve their educational performance.*' (Barton, 1998: 81)

Underpinning these developments has been a change in the welfare 'discourse' by which our commonsense understanding of education was to be shaped. The everyday language of the business world came to permeate the education policy debate: economy, efficiency and effectiveness; performance indicators and quality management systems; input, output and value-for-money measurements; and so forth:

> '*In this context education is increasingly viewed as a private as opposed to a public good. Schools need to be more business-like and by investing them with more decision-making powers, the pressure is towards forcing them to become more marketable and seriously concerned with their reputations*'. (Barton, 1998: 81)

The changing dominant discourse of welfare has permitted the legitimation of new forms of welfare administration and management - described as the rise of the New Public Management or NPM (Clarke and Newman, 1997). Key features of the NPM include decentralised cost centres, purchaser/provider splits, competition between providers, value for money and performance indicators. In attempting to explain this shift, Clarke *et al.* explore the values and beliefs shaping what they describe as the 'process of managerialization', values and beliefs that they term 'managerialism'. Effectively, Clarke *et al.* see managerialism as both an ideology '*that legitimizes and seeks to extend the "right to manage" and as composed of overlapping, and sometimes competing, discourses that present distinctive versions of "how to manage"*' (Clarke *et al.*, 2000: 9). Behaving in a business-like way, achieving value for money, and consistently striving for greater and greater cost savings have supplanted other management principles based on professional values, democratic accountability and social justice.

The impact of the Conservatives' reforms

The drive towards performance improvement in education in order to rise up league tables means that schools are facing enormous pressures. There is real concern that this compulsion may be exacerbating inequalities in the education system. For instance:

'The league tables have a clear, built-in bias against schools in disadvantaged areas, where educational performance is lower because socio-economic circumstances are worse. This bias is likely to increase inequality if schools adopt certain policies designed to try to push them up the league table. One way of doing this at the secondary level is for schools to concentrate their resources on pupils most likely to achieve exam success ... The pressures on school managers created by the league tables are not likely to be in the best interests of ... pupils in most need of extra attention.' (Plewis, 2000: 91)

At the same time, there is no clear evidence that the changes imposed by the Conservatives have produced significant, sustainable improvements in school standards. Walker and Stott, drawing on a parallel between performance-enhancing drugs in sport and performance-enhancing initiatives in education, argue:

'Schools have been both offered and "prescribed" performance stimulants. These substances have promised short-term success, but rarely produced any lasting, positive change in the classroom. They too have caused harmful side effects, and have contributed to a feeling of unease about the future of education'. (Walker and Stott, 2000: 63)

Notwithstanding doubts about the validity of official statistics (May 2001), OFSTED's own data demonstrates that between 1995 and 2000 the average total GCSE/GNVQ points score for 15-year-old pupils rose only very gradually - from 34.6 to 38.4 - while the rate of increase declined between 1999 and 2000 - from 38.0 to 38.4. In addition, while the proportion of pupils achieving five or more A-C grades rose gradually over the same period – from 41.2 to 47.4 per cent – the percentage of pupils attaining Level 5 or above in English at Key Stage 3 went into decline between 1999 and 2000 – from 64 to 63 per cent. Indeed, around one third of pupils do not improve their literacy or numeracy skills sufficiently to reach Level 5 by the end of Key Stage 3, impacting on pupils' progress across a range of subjects. Teaching quality is perceived as weaker in Key Stage 3 than in Key Stage 4. Furthermore, considerable variation in the average attainment of pupils in different schools continues, with pupils from schools with disadvantaged intakes suffering the most (OFSTED, 2001). These achievements are not particularly remarkable, a corollary to which is - have the costs been worth it? Walker and Stott suggest they have not:

'From a long-term perspective, neither the quality of student learning nor the capacity of teachers to improve their classroom skills had been affected. Indeed, reforms aimed at standards alone have been judged as largely unsuccessful.' (Walker and Stott, 2000: 66)

Moreover, as Chitty and Dunford (1999) argue, it has not been easy working in the state education sector since 1979. The 'failings' of schools have been widely publicised while teachers have generally been distrusted and exposed to increasing pressures. The increasing stress on teachers has led to disaffection and a crisis in teacher recruitment. Perhaps more significantly, the ethos about what education means appears to have changed:

> 'Many [school] principals became distracted from the core purposes of improving the quality of learning and the lives of the pupils because of the unfamiliar and overwhelming demands placed on them.'
> (Walker and Stott, 2000: 67)

Furthermore, we appear to have lost the comprehensive ideal of the post-war system that believed in 'the educability of all children ... regardless of their circumstances' (Chitty, 1999: 31) as a civil right. Instead, in the pursuit of some spurious notion of 'excellence', we appear to be erecting barriers to inclusive learning. As Chitty and Dunford observe:

> 'As the external pressures on schools have grown ... the number of pupils excluded from schools ... has grown by several hundred per cent.'
> (Chitty and Dunford, 1999: 7)

At the end of the Conservatives' 18 years in government, an estimated 100,000 children were temporarily excluded from school with another 13,000 permanently excluded (SEU, 1998), since which time 'the proportion of unsatisfactory behaviour is slightly higher' (OFSTED 2001: 7). Rising exclusions can be seen as a response by schools to the need 'to protect their reputations for discipline and good order locally' (Trowler, 1998: 19). While this problem may appear to affect a tiny fraction of the 8 million children in our schools, as Davies argues:

> 'The numbers conceal as much as they reveal. They say nothing about the children who are "cleansed" - pushed out of schools by headteachers who avoid officially recording them as exclusions. They say nothing about the children who turn up at school to be registered and then walk straight out. Most of all they ignore all the children who are out of school but who do not qualify to be counted ... students whose absence from school is authorised by parents who want them at home as carers for siblings ... [and those who] have fallen through the system, usually because of their families' unstable lives.' (Davies, 2000: 1)

It is within the context of this undermined and demoralised state school system that New Labour came to power in 1997 with a manifesto pledge to make education their number one priority.

Education policy and New Labour

The return of a Labour government in 1997 resulted in both continuity and change in British social policy. In some areas of policy, particularly New

Labour's stated commitment to social inclusion, there promised to be a different emphasis. On the other hand, there are numerous continuities with previous Conservative policies, such as the need for tight spending controls. This concern with cost containment has meant *'a consistent emphasis on 'no going back' to models of public service provision predicated on integrated professional bureaucracies'* (Clarke *et al.*, 2000: 15). Throughout all areas of welfare New Labour has retained, and in some cases extended, the managerial processes introduced under the Conservatives. In education, the national curriculum, league tables, 'naming and shaming' under-performing schools, selection and so forth have all been preserved. As Stuart Hall suggests:

> *'The framing strategy of New Labour's economic repertoire remains essentially the neo-liberal one ... [including] the wholesale refashioning of the public sector by the New Managerialism'.*
> (Hall (1998) cited in Burden *et al.*, 2000: 290)

Setting standards and performance targets remain central to New Labour's modernisation programme, meaning the business-model of education and competition between self-managing schools remain intact. Yet at the same time, New Labour is also pledged to tackle social exclusion in the name of social justice. As the Deputy Prime Minister John Prescott put it, in a speech to the Fabian Society/New Policy Institute Conference on 'Building Partnerships for Social Inclusion' held at Congress House on 15 January 2002:

> *'Something at the very heart of this Government's ambitions ... something I've fought for throughout my political career and still believe in passionately today ... is to combat poverty and social exclusion, and create a society of security and opportunity for all, where social justice prevails.'*

This assurance includes a commitment to promote social opportunity in education. Indeed, during his 1997 election campaign, Tony Blair was keen to stress:

> *'To those who say where is Labour's passion for social justice, I say education is social justice.'* (Tony Blair, *Times Educational Supplement* 18 April 1997, cited in Trowler, 1998: 93).

There is a clear tension here between, on the one hand, New Labour's neo-liberal economic orthodoxy (including maintaining quasi-markets in welfare) and, on the other, their 'Old' Labour (social democratic) espousal of social inclusion and opportunity. As various studies have shown, education markets polarise rather than equalise opportunities. Moreover, as we saw in Chapter 1, there is little evidence that New Labour is determined to remove socio-economic barriers to opportunity. In fact, income inequality in Britain widened during New Labour's first three years in government (National Statistics, 2002: 95).

New Labour's early strategy on school exclusion was founded on the principle of 'inclusivity' – that is, keeping pupils in mainstream school. They set a target for reducing exclusions by 30 per cent by 2002, to be achieved through a 'stick-and-carrot' approach. The carrot came in the form of funding through the *Excellence in Cities* programme and involved around 1000 schools in six metropolitan areas. This funding went towards establishing learning support units and mentoring schemes. The stick came in the form of loss of revenue when schools exclude a pupil. Davies identified three problems with New Labour's strategy: first, there was no clear consensus on how in-school support should be delivered; second, the mentoring system, where 'difficult' pupils are assigned a 'big brother' or 'sister', received heavy criticism in research conducted by the Centre for Social Action (CSA):

'The mentoring relationships created are too shallow to make a difference ... What is regrettable is seeing the potential of this form of practice wasted through insufficient planning, lack of money, lack of communication and lack of a philosophical base that values young people's participation.'
(CSA, cited in Davies, 2000: 6)

Third, the strategy to promote inclusivity in education is undermined by other areas of New Labour's social policy. The government's resolve to maintain the bulk of Conservative education reforms will do little, argues Davies, to address the difficulties faced by the most 'disaffected' children. In particular, schools now have an incentive to exclude children perceived to be 'difficult' during the initial selection process in order to boost their chances of attaining a higher position in the league tables. Leaving the Conservative reforms in place while introducing new measures to counter exclusion is contradictory. *'The problem is that neither structure provides a neutral framework in which a school can decide a child's future on grounds of education and behaviour'* (Davies, 2000: 6). The introduction of performance-related pay linked to results adds further incentive for teachers to resist the integration of 'difficult' pupils in their classrooms.

The government's new investment through *Excellence in Cities* also obscures simultaneous cutbacks. Previous provision - in the form of LEA pupil referral units (PRUs) or Behaviour Support Centres (BSCs) - is being substantially cut. BSCs would previously support truants, pregnant schoolgirls and young mothers, but this is no longer required under New Labour's reforms. Moreover, there is the possibility that some LEAs may seek to save funds by closing off-site support units, believing that the new in-school support centres will meet the government's targets. Sheffield LEA was planning to get rid of 16 per cent of its BSC staff and close its support for truants and pregnant girls, as well as reduce its support for pupils excluded for more than three weeks. It was placing an emphasis on the hitherto untried and challenging system of inclusive education (Davies, 2000).

Conclusions

A major change in education since the establishment of the post-war system has been a shift in emphasis. Notions about equality through education - no matter how limited, perhaps, in terms of the extent to which they succeeded in practice – seem increasingly irrelevant to politicians in the early twenty-first century. In many ways, schools and teachers have been held increasingly responsible for society's economic and social ills. In particular, the so-called 'progressive' education of the 1960s has been mythologised as a period when standards declined and young people failed to achieve the knowledge and skills needed for the world of work. At the same time, this was seen as a period when traditional 'decent' values, such as respect and discipline, broke down. Countering this attack is evidence that throughout the entire post-war period there has been little change in educational attainment standards in the state sector. The negative depiction of state schooling within dominant thinking, however, has created something close to a moral panic, leading many middle-class families to reject their local neighbourhood school and, in some cases, move house to a catchment area with a high performing school. This tendency, alongside the retention of internal markets and 'parental choice', is exacerbating exclusionary processes inherent in British society today (Burden *et al.*, 2000).

New Labour's Third Way is continuity with the neo-liberal way - effectively, the consolidation and extension of Thatcherism, reflected in Blair's post-2001 election pledge to extend the role of markets in education and health. As Coates and Brown argue:

> *'Since the Third Way is in fact a new partnership of Government and Big Business, of state and capital, the fine words about fairness and social justice are purely rhetorical. Effective markets mean the domination of the largest accumulations of capital and globalisation means that these will be primarily American. The instruments of globalisation – the World Bank, IMF and World Trade Organisation – will be employed to open up markets everywhere. In the past it was mining and manufacturing; today it is in the public utilities and services, and increasingly this will include all that social provision which we have come to rely upon in public hands – health, education, pensions, social security, housing, parks and pleasure grounds.'*
> (Coates and Barratt Brown, 2001: 19-20)

Consequently, Blair's stated commitment to 'education as social justice' looks a hollow assurance, as does his government's plan to promote 'community values' and democratic participation through citizenship education. As Tomlinson argues:

> *'Education markets did not encourage social balance in schools, equalize opportunities or help the socially excluded, and social segregation in*

education worked against the possibility of preparing good citizens who care about each other.' (Tomlinson, 2001: 169)

References

Barton, L. (1998) 'Markets, Managerialism and Inclusive Education', in P. Clough (ed) *Managing Inclusive Education: From Policy to Experience*, London: Paul Chapman Publishing, pp.78-91.

Burden, T., Cooper, C. and Petrie, S. (2000) *'Modernising' Social Policy: Unravelling New Labour's Welfare Reforms*, Aldershot: Ashgate.

Coates, K. and Barratt Brown, M. (2001) *Third Way ... Where to? – An exchange between Tony Blair, Ken Coates and Michael Barratt Brown*, Nottingham: Spokesman Books.

Chitty, C. (1999) 'The Comprehensive Ideal', in C. Chitty and J. Dunford (eds) *State Schools: New Labour and the Conservative Legacy*, London: Woburn Press, pp.19-32.

Chitty, C. and Dunford, J. (eds) (1999) *State Schools: New Labour and the Conservative Legacy*, London: Woburn Press.

Clarke, J., Gewirtz, S. and McLaughlin, E. (2000) *New Managerialism, New Welfare*, London: Sage.

Clarke, J. and Newman, J. (1997) *The Managerial State: Power, Politics and Ideology in the Remaking of Social Welfare*, London: Sage.

Davies, N. (2000) 'The tower block children for whom school has no point', *The Guardian*, 10 July, pp. 1, 6-7.

May, T. (2001) *Social Research: Issues, Methods and Process*, 3rd. Edition, Buckingham: Open University Press.

National Statistics (2002) *Social Trends No. 32*, London: The Stationery Office.

OFSTED (2001) *1999-2000 Standards and Quality in Education – The Annual Report of Her Majesty's Chief Inspector of Schools*, London: The Stationery Office.

Plewis, I. (2000) 'Educational inequalities and Education Action Zones', in C. Pantazis and D. Gordon (eds) *Tackling inequalities: Where are we now and what can be done?*, Bristol: Policy Press, pp. 87-100.

(SEU) Social Exclusion Unit (1998) *Truancy and School Exclusion Report by the Social Exclusion Unit*, London: Cabinet Office.

Tomlinson, S. (2001) *Education in a post-welfare society*, Buckingham: Open University Press.

Trowler, P. (1998) *Education Policy*, Eastbourne: Gildredge.

Walker, A. and Stott, K. (2000) 'Performance Improvement in Schools – A Case of Overdose', *Educational Management & Administration*, 28 (1), pp.63-76.

Chapter three

The perceptions of excluded pupils

Perceptions on their permanent exclusion

The pupils interviewed had been excluded for a range of reasons including the disruption of lessons and 'violent' conduct. In all cases, sanctions had been imposed prior to permanent exclusion - pupils had missed out on trips, been suspended, put in detention and/or isolated within the school. Glen stated that he was excluded for head-butting a teacher. He explained the reason for the attack was because the teacher had threatened him. He also claimed to have rammed a cup in the face of another teacher because he had called a black pupil *'nigger'*. He thought that his exclusion was unfair and felt that the school should have helped him manage his behaviour through, for example, counselling and anger management. Jack said he was excluded after kicking a teacher. He thought this was unfair because he *'didn't do it'*. He also said he had been in trouble at school before for fighting and had been temporarily excluded. Instead of exclusion Jack thought that the school could have simply *'phoned my mum and let me have detentions'*. William stated that his exclusion was due to an allegation that he had robbed a chemist shop. *'But I didn't do it. I was there at the time, but I was only watching'*. He thought the school head should have gone to the chemist and *'looked at the [CCTV] video ... He just picked and chose'*. William had previously been in trouble at school for allegedly scratching a car and attacking two boys, and suspended from school for throwing an object at a teacher. Cheryl said her exclusion followed a period of *'cheeking teachers'* and then one violent argument with a teacher. She thought her exclusion was unfair and felt *'picked-on'*. Instead of exclusion, she thought the school should have arranged a meeting with her and her father to discuss the matter.

Dave said he was excluded for hitting another pupil. He thought that this was fair because *'I had a meeting with the governors the night before and they told me if I get into any more trouble they're going to permanently exclude me'*. Dave says that he was not particularly bothered about being excluded because he *'hated school'*. He had previously been in trouble for being cheeky to teachers and hitting other pupils. Jeremy said he had been in a fight and the *'teacher phoned me up and said don't come back to school 'til you learn to mingle'*. He thought it unfair because *'it was after school. It had nothing to do with the teacher'*. Jeremy had been in trouble at school before the incident for *'fights, being cheeky to teachers'*. He felt that the school could have helped him more by having smaller classes, adding that larger classes left him feeling bored. Joanna said that she had been excluded for not following the school rules on wearing a uniform and jewellery. She said that she had been in trouble at school before for being '*a bit naughty ... not handing in homework ... watching a fight at school ... truancy ... Things like that ... But I wasn't terrible. I was OK'*. She didn't think her exclusion was fair, even though she acknowledged that she should not have been wearing jewellery. Nancy was excluded and sent to a Behaviour Support Centre (BSC) and was excluded from there after just three days. She was outside any structured schooling for about five months before returning to her original school in June 2000. She was excluded a second time the following September and was still out of school at the time of the interview (end of October 2000). She believed she had been excluded for getting into a fight, '*defending herself*' against a boy, and that this had been unfair as he was at fault as well. Nancy had been in trouble at school previously for talking and messing around in class, for which she had received detentions and put into isolation:

> '*Isolation is where you're in a room on your own. And you get set work from all the teachers and you're not allowed to look out and you're not allowed out. There's a toilet in the room, and they bring dinner to me*'.

On one occasion Nancy had been in isolation for three weeks. She had also been suspended from the school. She felt her exclusion had been unfair and caused mainly by boredom.

Reflections on their 'challenging behaviour'

In explaining his behaviour, Glen thought that it was connected to the violence he had experienced from an early age - both from his father (until his parents divorced) and at primary school where three teachers had '*beaten*' him: '*so, by the time I had reached secondary school, I hated teachers*'. Glen explained his own bullying of other children as due to being bullied himself by his father: '*bullies breed bullies*'. Given the opportunity to start his school career again, Glen stated that he would change '*everything*' about the way he behaved. In particular, he would have complained more about the teachers and worked harder.

Jack explained his behaviour as due to him finding some schoolwork difficult:

> '*Some of the work was hard and I used to get up and walk around and that, talk to my friends ... I used to ask them what they [the teachers] said ... I end up told off for asking questions and then ended up getting cheeky and I'd have to stand out of the room and the head teacher would have to warn me. I'd have to go down to the office and stuff like that*'.

Jack thought that this could have been avoided if he could have received more one-to-one tuition. '*There was this kid in my class called Baxter and, er, he got a teacher that sat in with him every lesson and helped him*'. It later transpired that Jack was dyslexic. When asked if he would behave differently if he could start his school career again Jack stated that he *'would not take the blame'* for trouble a second time.

William believed that his conflicts with teachers stemmed from their physical actions against him – being *'prodded and poked'*, often for trivial reasons such as the way he was sitting. Given the chance to start his school career again, William was not sure how he would have behaved differently. Cheryl thought her behaviour was due to feeling *'disliked'* by teachers. When asked if she would have changed anything about her behaviour Cheryl said *'I wouldn't have lost my temper'*.

Dave was not sure about the reasons for his behaviour, but went on to say:

'I don't get on with many people and plus the teachers are nasty too. You automatically fit if you like the teacher. I like art. I used to get on with the art teacher. I used to enjoy art and science 'cos I used to like the science teacher too'.

Dave said that if he were starting his school career again he would not change anything about his behaviour.

Jeremy thought that he behaved the way he did because he was *'bored and ... got in with a bad crowd'*. Given the chance to start his school career again, Jeremy stated that he would have behaved differently by *'being good'*. Joanna said she behaved in the way she did *'to show off to my friends, to look big. That was more why I did it'*. Given a second chance to start her school career, Joanna was in two minds about behaving differently because:

'some of the things I've done aren't wrong but I still got into trouble for them. But yeah, I think I am sorry. I wish I hadn't got expelled ... I think I should have got on with my work and done what I ought to have done instead of trying to show off in front of my friends. And I should have got home and done my work'.

Nancy thought that she had become *'rebellious'* out of boredom:

'Well, I do my work fast and I sit and talk and that when some will have finished their work. But there are some who haven't, and I'd get in trouble 'cos they hadn't finished their work and they're talking to me'.

Given the chance to start her school career again, Nancy said that she would have tried to change her behaviour. *'If I knew what was going to happen when I got excluded – if I'd known all along – then I would have concentrated on the way my attitude was'.*

Perceptions on the exclusion process

Glen felt that he was given opportunity to express his views prior to being excluded. He did not feel, however, that the school was responsive to his needs: *'I told them I asked for help and didn't get it. I told them "you couldn't be bothered". But they did not like what I said'.* Jack felt that he had had no voice during the exclusion process:

> *'They said "go home" and then you come back on the Wednesday. And then I got a letter – "you're permanently excluded" – saying that and that what happened. And then my mum phoned up and she said that she was sick and she couldn't go to the [exclusion] meeting and they just carried on without us'.*

William and Cheryl also felt that they did not have an opportunity to express their views during the exclusion process. In contrast, Dave felt that he had been given an opportunity to be involved, and thought the decision to exclude him fair. Jeremy could not remember the exclusion process. Joanna remembered a meeting where she was invited to say how she felt. *'I says that I shouldn't have done the things I did'.* Nancy did not feel she had given the opportunity to express herself during the exclusion process, adding:

> *'Well, you say something to the teachers and they say, "you're only 14, I'm not speaking to you" ... They say to "respect your elders", but they don't give us respect. So why should we give them respect if they don't listen to you. And the other point was they all want to put you down and that. And they're butting in when I'm speaking. I get angry with it really. I just want to make them listen, and I used to shout at them and then just walk off. They just wind me up'.*

Experiences following exclusion

Glen said that it was three months before he found a place in a BSC and that during that time he had not been given schoolwork to do. He spent most of the time playing on his computer at home. Jack stated that it was six to eight weeks before he went to a BSC and that during this time he *'watched telly ... cleaned the house'.* He wasn't given any schoolwork to do:

> *'They [the school] weren't really bothered. They never phoned up and said "here you are, we'll send you some work out for you to do while you're not at school"'.*

William said it was three to four months before he found a place at a BSC, during which time he did receive some home tuition. Cheryl was luckier in that, within a few days, she was back in a mainstream school. She added *'I like my new school better. The teachers are better'.* Dave said he was four to five months out of school before finding a place at a BSC. During this time he *'stayed in, read books, talked to my mates, listened to music'.* Jeremy said it was about six months before he found a place at a BSC, during which time he received no schoolwork and mainly watched television. Joanna was just three weeks out of school before getting into a BSC. Nancy spent her days after exclusion visiting school friends during their lunch breaks, going to the shops, visiting her mother, watching TV and playing on her computer.

The pupil respondents described their feelings following exclusion. Glen had felt *'very low for a while ... a failure. Now I feel lazy ... demotivated. I feel that I won't be able to do what I want to do in the future'*. Jack stated that he felt *'hurt and upset all in one go'*. He said that *'because it had never happened to me before I was scared in case some police or something would take me away'*. William stated that he felt *'depressed'*. Cheryl stated that she *'missed her friends'*. Similarly, Joanna stated that she felt upset *'more 'cos I wasn't gonna see my friends anymore. I think it was more that then upset 'cos I'm not in school'*. Jeremy stated that he felt *'lonely'*. In contrast, Dave stated that he felt *'quite happy ... 'cos I got to go to the Bridge Centre (a BSC)'*. Nancy felt:

> *'upset at first ... I was trying to behave, I was trying. But they didn't understand at all. They just think, "oh, she just doesn't do what we say". I couldn't win anyway ... They could have just suspended me. They could have put me on isolation as well. But they went too far in excluding me'.*

Perceptions on the effectiveness of exclusion

Glen did not think exclusion was an effective way of changing behaviour. He felt that schools should use the sanction of *'ignoring bad, rewarding good ... instead of pupils paying for trips they could get merit awards for good behaviour and use these towards them'*. He also thought schools should offer pupils help to deal with their anger:

> *'They did not help me enough ... I wanted to see the school nurse [who was a psychologist] ... I needed counselling, anger management ... They could have contacted the Behaviour Support Service sooner ... and helped me with my situation'.*

Similarly, Cheryl felt that she had needed help from the BSC to deal with her anger instead of being excluded. Jeremy also thought that the school should have helped him, but *'they never used to bother with me, pissing on me they were'*. Jack felt that pupils could be given detention or made to attend school on Saturdays or Sundays instead of exclusion. William felt that pupils could be given more practical things to do, like fix old cars. Dave did not think permanent exclusion was an answer, though did not know what else to suggest. Only Joanna thought that exclusion might help to change behaviour: *'yes, depends on some people 'cos some people can get expelled and then go down to a special unit and that could be even worse. But I've changed 'cos I don't want to get expelled again'*. Nancy was not sure permanent exclusion was an effective way of changing pupils' behaviour, though she acknowledged that it had taught her to *'realise how important that education is, and if I didn't do these things then I would still be there'*.

Perceptions on the City's Behaviour Support Service

Glen felt that one particular BSC teacher was able to identify with him. He also appreciated the BSC's flexible rules and system of privileges for rewarding good behaviour (for instance, going to McDonalds or skiing). Jack felt that he has benefited from being at a BSC. *'I made friends and they helped me ... Mr X [a BSC head] said "don't be afraid to stand up to what people say"'*. Jack also felt, however, that he did not spend enough time at the centre (only two hours for four days a week) and that it had given the wrong impression to his brothers. *'We went rock climbing and caving and that, and my brothers said "ah, that's not fair. If we be naughty we might be able to do all that stuff"'*. William felt that the BSC had given him an opportunity to *'make new friends ... and have a fresh start'*. Dave felt he had benefited from being at a BSC because:

> *'you only had a couple of hours a day ... you had four days a week and it weren't hard. They weren't strict and if you needed help then they'd help yer 'cos there's not many in a classroom. It just, well, they get round a lot. There's about four of you in a class or two mainly so you get more attention'*.

Joanna felt that she had benefited from the BSC because there she *'had someone to talk to'*. Jeremy did not feel that he had benefited from the BSC, saying that it had been *'boring ... the lessons. English on Monday and Art and something else on a Tuesday'*. Nancy, who had been excluded from a BSC after three days, did not believe it had benefited her. Cheryl had been reintegrated directly back into a mainstream school.

Perceptions on schools and teachers

Glen stated that he most enjoyed school in Year 8 because he did not get into trouble. *'But then I changed, because of trouble with my dad'*. He disliked school the most in Year 9 when he got into trouble with the teachers. He was particularly critical of the way pupils' files (transferred from school to school with the pupil) are used. *'These files should be banned ... teachers use them against you. Once you have a bad reputation it follows you'*. Jack most enjoyed school when he had *'PE and been with all my friends 'cos the PE teacher used to play with us, pick us up, and throw us and that'*. Jack disliked English lessons the most:

> *"cos the teacher used to always pick on me ... I think the English teacher was old fashioned ... She used to shout at me and she used to try and put me down in the lesson in front of everyone. And then I just ended up shouting at her and that's how I got thrown out of my lessons. She used to try and*

call me names in the lesson but say it in a smart way so that everyone laughed ... She try to do it to everyone ... She tries to discipline the class by making people look stupid'.

William most enjoyed school when he did science subjects, partly because of the teachers. What he most disliked about school was the head teacher who *'didn't care'*. Cheryl mostly liked Maths and Art, and mostly disliked PE and History (because of the teachers). Dave mostly enjoyed Science, Art and English, his *'best subjects'*. What he says he disliked most was Maths, Design Technology, IT and French. *'I did like DT, but I didn't get on with the teacher. French, I just couldn't do the lesson, I just couldn't do it'*. Jeremy said that there was nothing at all about school he enjoyed. *'I just hated school basically'*. Joanna stated that she liked:

> *'most lessons ... I did like school but some of the teachers I didn't like ... they were always watching you ... I couldn't go anywhere. There was a certain teacher that was always - 'cos he's like head of our Year - he's always watching us and following me around. I couldn't really do anything 'cos if I did one little thing wrong I'd be straight up before the head teacher ... If I had the wrong coloured socks on or something he was gonna tell the head teacher'.*

Nancy most enjoyed Maths because of the subject. What she disliked most was the lack of respect from the teachers and French *'cos it's hard to understand'*.

Glen described a 'good' teacher as:

> *'someone who listens to you ... teachers should be themselves, a normal person, have a sense of humour, have respect for us and not lash out ... [and be] well-trained so as to manage me ... They should not just dish out punishment but ask "why" kids behave the way they do'.*

He thought that teachers *'picked-on kids for silly reasons'* such as not wearing a school uniform. He felt that he had been picked-on, and that this had made him feel even more angry: *'being blamed and criticised by teachers all the time – on top of being blamed and criticised by parents at home – becomes too much'*. Glen described a 'bad' teacher as someone with *'no understanding of or interest in pupils'*. He also believed that some teachers were racist and that some were liars who would fabricate pupil reports to the Governors.

Jack described a 'good' teacher as one who *'joked'*. He described a 'bad' teacher as one who would use ridicule to discipline a class. Jack felt that the attitude of the teacher is more important than the subject itself in relation to whether he enjoyed lessons or not. William described a good teacher as someone with personality and caring, a bad teacher as *'plain awful'*. Cheryl described a 'good' teacher as someone who *'cares, listens and helps'* and a 'bad' teacher as someone who does not. Dave described a 'good' teacher as *'someone who talks to you, says hello and helps you if you're having problems'*. He described a 'bad' teacher as the opposite. Jeremy used similar definitions, but also thought that a 'good' teacher was someone who *'just has something about them'*. Joanna described a 'good' teacher as someone who was *'understanding and fair'* and had a sense of humour. *'It's not very good when you've just got a teacher who just sets you work ... and don't speak to you'*. A 'good' teacher is one *'who gets involved and sits down with you'*. A 'bad' teacher is one *'who would just set you work and just get you to get on with ... They won't come and help you or enjoy it with you or do stuff with you'*. Nancy described a 'good' teacher as someone like:

> *'Mr E, 'cos he listens, he understands, and he gives you as much fun as you need. He's interesting, yeah. On the day I thought I was getting excluded I was in his office crying. I knew they wanted me out and he went and got me a box of tissues and that'.*

Nancy described a 'bad' teacher as someone who *'doesn't listen to you. They don't give you any respect'*.

Pupil respondents described experiences of being 'picked-on' by teachers. Glen stated that teachers had pushed him and that this had inflamed his anger. Jack had felt humiliated by a teacher in class and this had made him shout back. William said that a teacher had hit him across the face and that this is now the subject of legal proceedings. Cheryl felt picked-on by being (wrongly in her view) accused of fighting, even though the teacher *'couldn't even see me'*. Jeremy felt picked-on by one particular teacher, even though it was often *'other kids messing around'*. Joanna had felt picked-on because of her past. *'I know that if I didn't have a history of getting into trouble then they wouldn't have to watch me'*. Nancy had felt picked-on by *'loads'* of teachers. Only Dave felt that he had not been picked-on. *'No, I wouldn't let anyone pick on me, even a teacher. I'd shout back at them and ... mess up the lessons'*.

What Glen would most like to change about schools is *'the way teachers teach ... what they teach ... and the number of lessons'*. He said lessons should be *'more fun and interesting'*. Jack did not really know what he would like to change about school or teachers but, like Glen, thought that the teacher was more important than the subject in respect of whether he enjoyed a lesson or not. William did not know how he would change school, but added that he felt that a combination of an interesting subject and a good teacher were important in respect of his enjoyment of classes. Cheryl most wanted to change schools by stopping exclusions and changing the *'bad teachers'*. She again thought that the most important factor for the enjoyment of lessons was the teacher. Jeremy would change schools by getting in better teachers, adding that teachers were important in terms of whether classes were enjoyable. Dave wanted to change the rules, teachers and attendance times in school. He thought schools should start and finish later. As for bad teachers, he stated *'I wouldn't change them, I'd just kick 'em out'*. Joanna was not sure about how to change schools but emphasised the importance of teachers in relation to the enjoyment of classes. She enjoyed PE, Drama and Art because the teachers were *'more free ... There's a lot more space. You could say what you wanted to say ... It was just something different from English, Maths and Science'*. Nancy wanted to change the attitude of teachers most: *'I'd like the teachers to give more respect to you, give you more attention'*.

Most of the pupils were aware of the school rules and found them to be 'sensible'. Only Jeremy claimed that he did not know what the school rules were, while Dave felt that some of the rules should have been more positive. *'They were all "no, you can't do this; no, you can't do that"'*. None of the respondents felt that they had an opportunity to express their own views on the rules shaping how their school was managed. In the case of Dave, *'no. No schools are like that really, are they?'*.

Perceptions on neighbourhood, family and friends

Glen stated that he generally liked living in his neighbourhood:

> *'I'm used to it ... been here most of my life ... It's rough, living on the edge where you have to learn fast ... My friends are here ... I feel safe most of the time. And there's the availability of the things I need – drink, weapons, drugs, etc. And I can learn about music – people are always playing music (garage, hip-hop, etc.)'*.

Glen did dislike the lack of facilities in the area, and the fact that you were *'labelled and stigmatised'* living in this part of the City. He also felt that there were not enough police, and too much crime and violence: *'I do feel anxious for my own safety some times'*. Glen said that he spent his leisure time visiting his friends' houses: *'hanging around ... chatting ... going to the park'*. All his friends were older than him - he had no friends his own age. He said that nobody wanted to use the youth clubs in the area (*'youth clubs don't work'*) and thought that there should be arranged trips to places. When asked who was most important to him in his life Glen was reluctant to answer, other than to say that he had *'two special friends'*. Glen's role model in life is John Claude Van Damme (*'a great sex god'*). The person he most dislikes in the world is his *'real dad'*.

What Jack most liked about his neighbourhood was friends, the local park, the youth club, the football pitch and the convenience (bus routes, shops, etc.). The things he most disliked about his neighbourhood were the canal (*'I can't swim ... [and] its dirty and there's rats around it'*), the prison (*'someone might escape'*), litter and pollution, drugs, the shops serving under-aged kids with cigarettes and car crime. Jack had once run away from home because he was unhappy, but *'only to my nans ... Me and my nan got on good'*. Jack met his friends outside or at the park. He liked to play football. The thing he felt would most improve his life was having his own bedroom (he shares with his brothers). Jack said he felt happy at home and that his family was the most important thing in his life *"cos they're with me all the time'*. The person Jack most admired and wanted to be like was Michael Owen. The person he disliked the most was *'the woman round the corner ... 'cos she phones the police on us then, when we're walking past her door, if we're talking loud she says we're shouting at her and she just hates kids'*.

William liked his neighbourhood because of the *'atmosphere, friends, shops and the girls'*. The things he disliked the most were *'litter, violence and crime – guns and so on'*. He usually met his friends on the street where they often played football. He generally felt happy living at home with his mother, brother and sister. William most admired, and wanted to be like one day, Mike Cassidy. He disliked *'no-one'*. Cheryl liked where she lived because of the youth clubs, park and the proximity to town, and said that she felt happy living at home. There was nothing about the neighbourhood she disliked. She would spend her leisure time with friends who would visit her at home or go with her to McDonalds or the park. Cheryl could not suggest anything to improve life in her neighbourhood. The most important person in Cheryl's life is her dad because *'he understands me'*. There was nobody in the world Cheryl admired and wanted to be like.

Dave did not know if he liked the area he lived in – he had only been there three-and-a-half months. He had met people there already: *'I'm good at socialising'*. He meets his friends in the street or they come to his house. *'We hang around 'cos there's nothing round here'*. When asked what would improve the neighbourhood Dave replied: *'I'd like a big sports centre thing with a swimming pool in there'*. Dave felt happy living at home with his carer and her family. He stated that the most important person in his life is his sister (who lives with his mother) because *'she's my sister'*. The person Dave most admired was his uncle who lives in Tenerife. *'He's nice to know. He's not hurt anybody, he's got loads of friends, got his own business and he's done real well for himself'*. The people Dave disliked the most were *'boys (from his old school) 'cos they hit people'*.

Jeremy said that there was nothing he liked about his neighbourhood and that there was nothing to do there. He meets his friends in the streets and they find a pitch to play football on. The most important person in Jeremy's life is *'my mum ... 'cos she's my mum'*. When asked who in the world did he most admire Jeremy said *'the SAS'*. When asked who in the world he disliked the most he said *'the police ... 'cos they pick on me like'*. Joanna did not like the neighbourhood she lived in because *'there's nothing to do. That's why half the kids round here are naughty 'cos there's nothing'*. Her friends would normally come round to her house. When asked what she normally did with her friends Joanna replied: *'Well, I'm usually grounded but, erm, if I do see them I usually go to my friend's house ... We usually play a game or watch TV or listen to music. Or we just go down the shop. Anything really'*. When asked if she was happy living at home Joanna replied *'we have arguments, but yes'*. When asked who in the world she most admired and wanted to be like one day Joanna replied '*my mum*'. When asked who she most disliked Joanna replied '*erm, don't know, err … I think it's the teacher at school. It's just that I didn't like the way she used to treat me. She used to get me out in class and embarrass me in front of my friends*'. Nancy liked where she lived and '*the people in the lane*'. She would meet her friends after school and go to one of their houses where they would watch sport on television or play games on computer. '*Sometimes we sit down and talk about things to do with school*'. The most important person in Nancy's life is her '*mum. My dad left home, but my mum's always there for me*'. When asked who in the world she most admired, Nancy replied that she did not think about that. The person in the world she most disliked was another pupil, '*this girl I had a fight with ages ago … She's just all fake*'.

Future aspirations

Glen's ambition is to join the army or, failing that, to study to be a carpenter, plumber or some other trade at college. He would like to marry and have a child. When asked if he thought he would achieve these things Glen replied '*I don't really know … I feel having been thrown out of school has affected me*'. Glen considered his exclusion from school to be the main barrier preventing him from achieving his ambitions. On leaving school, Jack wants to be a builder, mechanic or carpenter. '*I might achieve a builder or a carpenter … I don't know about a mechanic*'. Jack was worried that his exclusion might impact on his career prospects '*because when I go to get a job they'll look back to my school records and see how I missed Year 8 and say "you can't have this job 'cos you might do this or that in your job"*'. William's long-term ambition is to go to college and study motor mechanics and computers. He wants to work with cars and believes he can achieve this ambition. Cheryl stated that she wants to become a hairdresser and feels that she will achieve this. She added that she did not want to get married. Dave's ambition is to go and live in Tenerife and work for his uncle or on his own. '*I'd like to go all round the world*'. When asked if he thought he could achieve these ambitions Dave replied '*yeah, if I put my mind to it – definitely!*'. Jeremy's ambition is to join the army. He is not sure he will be qualified for this though. Joanna's ambition is to '*go to college or university [and become] a dance instructor or an air hostess and travel countries and then, after that, I'd like to settle down and have a family*'. The main barrier she sees to achieving her ambition is '*if I get expelled again - [laughs] - but that's not gonna happen*'. Nancy wants to be '*a counsellor, 'cos I know loads of things that people go through. Otherwise, a fitness instructor*'. She also wants to be married with three children. She believes she will achieve the latter, but is not sure about the former due to the uncertainty of getting back into school.

Key issues raised

All the pupil respondents (except one) described their exclusion as unjust. In the case of the one exception, Dave, he claimed to have hated school and was glad to have been released. While many of the respondents acknowledged that they might have displayed 'challenging' behaviour in school, they did offer explanations for this that could have been responded to differently: child abuse; difficulty with schoolwork (in one case dyslexia); perceived disrespect from teachers; boredom; peer-group pressure. The respondents perceived different experiences of the exclusion process, from non-involvement to involvement. Those who claimed involvement largely felt that governors were unresponsive to their views or needs. Only Dave stated that he believed that his involvement had led to a 'fair' conclusion – his exclusion!

Following exclusion most of the respondents experienced difficulty re-entering a structured education programme. Many were out of the education system for three to six months, often without having schoolwork set. Most of the respondents experienced profound negative feelings after exclusion: failure; demotivation; pain; fear; depression; loneliness. Only Dave appeared to have felt positive! Most of the respondents thought exclusion is not an effective way of changing behaviour. A number of alternatives to school exclusion were suggested: sanctions and rewards; anger-management counselling; smaller class sizes; one-to-one tuition; detentions; weekend attendance; and more practical activities (such as car maintenance). One respondent, Joanna, thought exclusion might help in dealing with behaviour issues if it was combined with support from a special centre. Most pupil respondents were quite positive about the special provision received from the City's Behaviour Support Service's BSCs, the reasons being: empathetic teachers; flexible rules and systems of privileges; meeting new friends; offering a fresh start; and small class sizes allowing more attention. One respondent, Jack, felt that the BSC he attended offered insufficient time (just two hours, four days a week). One other, Jeremy, felt bored at the BSC he attended.

Describing their experiences of schools and teachers, most respondents highlighted the attitude of the teacher as the key factor determining their enjoyment or otherwise of school. In defining the characteristics of a 'good' teacher, respondents highlighted: humour; respect; good classroom management skills; empathy; caring; non-racist; good listening skills; understanding; fairness; enthusiasm. In defining the characteristics of a 'bad' teacher respondents highlighted mainly 'opposites': disrespect; poor classroom management skills; non-empathy; uncaring; racist; doesn't listen; unfairness; lack of enthusiasm. Most of the respondents had felt picked-on by teachers: pushed and poked; humiliated; struck across the face; wrongly accused. Only Dave felt he had not been picked-on. What most respondents most wanted to change about school was the way teachers taught. Dave suggested sacking bad teachers and having a shorter teaching day. The respondents generally agreed with the school rules. Only Dave felt that they could have been more positive. None of the respondents believed that they had had a role to play in shaping the way that their school was managed.

The respondents generally expressed positive experiences about their neighbourhood, family and friends. Some highlighted, however, profound anxieties that included: lack of facilities; feeling their residential area was labelled and stigmatised; crime and violence; litter and pollution; drugs. Glen's comments about the availability of drink, weapons, drugs, etc. – things he needed – are particularly telling. Most of the respondents had clear aspirations for the future: a trade, the army or further/higher education; and marriage and raising children. Whilst some remained optimistic about fulfilling these aspirations, others were concerned that their exclusion from school would prove to be a major barrier to their achievement.

Chapter four

The perceptions of parents/carers

Perceptions on their child's permanent exclusion

Grace (Glen's mother) stated that her son's exclusion had followed a number of incidents (34 cases of abusive language and violence had been recorded by the school). She felt, however, that he had been picked-on, particularly by one senior teacher *'who had it in for Glen all along'*. She alleged that he had been *'poked by a teacher for not wearing a uniform ... being late ... talking ... or leaving his coat on the back of a chair'*. She also felt that the school should have given him more support before his exclusion - particularly preventative action such as anger management. She claimed to have offered to support her son in school herself by sitting in the class with him or coming to the school when he was in trouble. Grace felt that *'the school had no respect for him ... They were waiting for an excuse to get rid of him. They did not want him to behave well ... Didn't want to find a solution ... They had given up on him'*. Jenny (Jack's mother) felt that her son's trouble at school had been for *'minor things ... fighting in the playground ... flooding toilets'*. She thought that the real cause of his problems was undiagnosed dyslexia. *'They sent him to the centre when he was in Year 7 - a care centre - because he was behind on all his work. They found out that he was dyslexic - he needed extra help but he wasn't getting it at school'*. Jenny went on to explain:

> *'Jack is in the classroom. They're all there. They're told to do a piece of work. He [the teacher] explains it and if Jack asks for it to be explained a second time he says, "oh, you didn't listen the first time so just get on with it". So, if a child can't do something, there's no point in sitting there trying 'cos he can't do it. There's no use saying "you've got to sit there" when he can't do it. That's why he messes about in the classroom, 'cos they didn't give him the help he needed'.*

Winnie (William's mother) thought that her son's exclusion for alleged theft of a chemist shop was unfair because it was based on insufficient evidence. Sheila (Cheryl's mother) was told that her daughter's exclusion was due to her smoking. *'But when I asked the teacher if they saw her smoking ... he said "no" and I said "well, how can you exclude her when you never saw her smoking?". "Erm", he said'*. Sheila added that Cheryl had been in trouble at school prior to her exclusion, but felt that this had been for:

> *'a few little things. Whenever anything happened at school they were picking on Cheryl ... An incident that took place ... they were throwing bits of glue into hair and stuff ... When they checked it all out, Cheryl had*

nothing to do with it. But they were suspending her. So I said, "well, why are you suspending her for something that she hasn't even done?" ... I'm thinking, why are they picking on her constantly all the time? She hasn't done anything wrong'.

Diane (Dave's carer) was not with Dave when he was excluded for fighting and bad behaviour, but *'Dave told me all about it ... I think he's got a bit of a temper on him sometimes but I think that's not as bad as it used to be ... Personally I don't have any problems with Dave'.* Joan (Jeremy's mother) said that her son was excluded for *'a fight outside school ...It was actually outside the school after school hours'* and that she thought that this was not really fair. *'It just seems they were picking on him. They just don't like him. You can tell ... I mean, the things Jeremy did and got suspended for ... He had one little fight with a kid and, er, he punched a girl's boob'.* Jim (Joanna's father) said his daughter's exclusion was for *'messing with her hair in class, talking, late for class - you know, nothing drastic. We're not talking about somebody who burnt the school down or knifed the teacher. But just, over a period of two years, continually niggling away at the system'.* He felt that the school's decision was fair – not for the final occasion (messing with hair and talking) but because it was the culmination of two years of incidents. Having said this, Jim and his wife had tried to persuade the school to give them support:

'We have as many problems here as they do at school ... Joanna is permanently grounded. We have enough arguments, scraps ... She is not our favourite around the house by any means ... Having said that, credit where it's due. She's doing well at the new school. So for that I'm grateful. I just wish she'd done it earlier, and we wouldn't have to have gone through all this process. That's perhaps another point. An option that I offered the governors [was]...let's just get on with the process of getting her into a new school and maybe getting us some help 'cos what we kept saying to the school over the last 18 months is "we can't change her, we're having as much trouble as you are ... We need some help"'.

Another option Jim asked for was for Joanna to attend a BSC (where she would receive counselling and, perhaps, the help of a child psychologist) while remaining at school:

'Not being familiar with the system, never having to deal with it before, we thought "well maybe that will help - maybe she will get some professional assistance and maybe we will". So I actually offered it to the headmistress before the governors meeting, and offered it to the governors at the meeting. "Why can't she stay at the school and be on a BSC's headcount ... dually assigned without actually been expelled ... If she doesn't improve while she's getting that help then by all means - I can understand the school's point of view, they don't want a disruptive child jeopardising other children's education - move her to another school"'.

However, Jim stated that the school governors rejected this option. He felt that impending changes at the time (the introduction of bursaries - *'severe financial penalties'* - paid for by schools who choose to exclude 'disruptive' pupils) encouraged schools to have a *'clear out'* of potentially difficult pupils before the new measures took effect. He also felt that the process of exclusion does not offer opportunities for contrition and forgiveness. *'As a child, how does she then work her way out of that? Even if she wants to, there doesn't appear to be any way back'.* He also felt that once a child has been excluded they face extreme pressure to demonstrate that they have reformed:

> *'Hopefully, the exclusion is going to sort her school problems out. She is doing better [at the new school]. It is early days, and she's fully aware that she's on trial. The telling point for me will be after they've said "yes" [she has reformed]. You know then that a little bit of the focus goes away from her, and she's just another member of the community'.*

Nina (Nancy's mother) stated that her daughter was excluded for fighting. She thought that the school's decision to exclude was too extreme. *'I think it was wrong. I mean, to be punished, fair enough. But not to go to that extreme - to kick her out'.* Nina said that her daughter had been in trouble at school before her exclusion but that this was *'just basically disruption in class ... Basically it was just her behaviour inside the classroom, that's she's a disruptive child. But they forgot to mention that she'd done all her work first. But the others were going along with her so they called her a bad influence and disruptive'.* Nina described some of the prior sanctions the school had imposed on her daughter: *'She would spend weeks in isolation, constantly on report ... They told me on numerous occasions that it would be best if Nancy left and, erm, they were always telling her that as well. They just didn't give her a chance to try and change her attitude'.*

Perceptions on the exclusion process

Grace felt that she had little or no involvement in the decision to exclude her son. She stated that she was called to a pre-exclusion meeting with the school head, a school governor, an LEA representative and a senior teacher. She described the experience as *'like being in court'*, yet she felt she had little or no support to help her defend her son. She did get some help from an education social worker and *'a woman from the exclusion section'* who told her about the City's Behaviour Support Service.

Jenny stated that the meeting that decided her son's exclusion was conducted without her:

> *'They had a meeting and they decided to get rid of Jack ... I wasn't well that week. I phoned up, said I couldn't make it, but they went ahead and had the meeting without me ... They didn't give him a fair hearing either*

because they said, going on other children's hearsay, that Jack kicked teacher. But the teacher didn't see Jack kick her so it was all hearsay. Just because Jack was in the middle of the crowd when it happened he got the blame'.

Winnie stated that she had attended an exclusion meeting but was not asked for her views and received no support. She felt her son had just been *'abandoned'*. Sheila felt that she had no say over the decision to exclude her daughter. She stated that, prior to her exclusion, Cheryl had:

'had about one day off a month. I told them she will have before she started, and they asked "why" and I said, "she has acute menstrual pain". She gets a lot of pain. If she's in a lot of pain she can't go, and they were using this - that she's hardly at school'.

Sheila was visibly angry talking about her daughter's treatment at school:

'I am angry to a certain extent, and to a certain extent I'm not 'cos I'm looking at it from the view that she's better off out of that school 'cos if they are gonna keep on picking on her for things she hasn't done then she should be out of there and somewhere where she will enjoy being. She's enjoying where she is now [back in another school]'.

Joan and Jeremy had attended meetings with the school prior to the decision to exclude, but Joan did not feel these were particularly helpful. *'I just don't think she [the head] wanted to know. I went to every meeting. It was more like, you know, "if he does it again he's out". They weren't listening to us'.* Jim and his wife thought that once the exclusion process was in train then it was almost unstoppable:

'As we said to the governors at the last session [exclusion meeting], we felt that the school had worked through a process and, probably 12 months into it, the decision had already been taken. And that they would then just follow the process ... The lowest point was 12 months before when, I think, there were three or four incidents over wagging it ... one they got caught in town and I think at that point the decision had been made that the school, unless there was some dramatic change, would just follow the process'.

Realising the situation:

'Our problem was convincing Joanna we knew what was gonna happen if she carried on down that road. The biggest problem I've got with the whole process is ... that there was no way back. It was almost like she was a totting-up process for demerits. But there was no way of gaining some merits to counteract them. She just, over a period of two years, totted-up points'.

Jim felt that there should be opportunities for pupils to make amends for 'bad' behaviour by setting them targets. *'Why can't we say "if you can stay out of trouble for a week we'll take some points off" ... give her something to work towards ... But there isn't a process for it'.* Nina felt that there was little point in trying to defend her daughter against the school's decision to exclude:

'When she was excluded I was just given a letter. There was a governor's report they sent me ... I suppose I could have gone in front of the committee. But I just thought I just couldn't be bothered anymore. I didn't want to, I don't think, 'cos, even if she had gone back in the school, they would never have left her alone'.

Nina had felt very stressed and worn down by the process:

'Every time the phone rings - I mean, I've got caller display and I knew who it was. And I just thought "what now!" When trouble kicked off she got the blame. Might not have had anything to do with her. She might have been there, round and about on the scene, but if she was accused and, of course, I wasn't there, I can't prove anything ... Very stressful, very stressful. Really wore me down in the end. I just didn't want to know anymore'.

Nina had sought the help of OFSTED, but believed that this had rebounded on her:

'I went to OFSTED and I said "we'd had a bit of trouble when she first started running away and, erm, why she was having trouble at school". I told the teachers this and, when I had the report - what the governors sent - they used it against me. And I thought "that's out of order" ... The way they worded it, the tone of the report and the way it was written, it was as if they'd used it against me: "Well, her mother can't control her. She's out of control" ... I just felt I trusted them and they just used it against me. There was no need for that to even be in the report, what I told them. In the end I just didn't care ... I said I'm not going to the governors' meeting'.

Nina also felt that she did not get any personal support when Nancy was being excluded. *'No, I didn't personally get any support at all ... They didn't care'.*

Experiences following exclusion

Grace stated that following her son's exclusion:

'He became isolated from his peer group and now finds it difficult making relationships with girls ... He has very low self-esteem and gets depressed ... he was on anti-depressants at one time ... He has no real idea of what he now wants to do and is put off going to college ... He feels stigmatised and says "What shall I say if they [college] ask me about school?" He has no exam passes'.

The three months Glen was out of school meant that Grace was stuck at home too; she could not trust Glen to be on his own and needed to know what he was up to. *'This got me depressed, although I did get some support from my mum who lives close by'*. Jenny stated that the period after Jack's exclusion was a time of great distress, confusion and fear for all the family. She felt left on her own to sort out what support would be available for Jack:

> *'What I'd done was, when I found out he was excluded, I phoned the headmaster in charge and he said, "someone will get in touch with you". So I sat here for two days and I cried and I cried about it. And then I decided I'd phone up a school and I said "what would happen if a child got excluded and all that" and she gave me a number to ring and it was the educational board. And then, when I got in touch with them, they put me in touch with another office and it was them who helped me. It took ages before he went to a centre [BSC]. I was worried that social services were going to come to the door and try and take him off me 'cos I wasn't sending him to school'.*

On a more positive note Jenny stated that the experience of Jack's exclusion had improved their relationship. *'We get on better now than we've ever done. We talk all the time. I tell him everything and he tells me everything. Well, I think he tells me everything'*. Winnie stated that William's exclusion caused him to lose *'respect for himself'* and caused her *'stress - I worry that he will never get back into school'*. She also sees his exclusion as *'a label he'll always have'*. She now tries to ensure William does not get in with a 'bad crowd'.

Sheila felt that she received little support following Cheryl's exclusion. *'The school didn't even talk to me about it. No, they just excluded her and that's that. No feedback, nothing explained. Why, no one came and talked to us about it'*. The only support she did receive was a visit from the head of one of the BSCs. In the end, however, Sheila found Cheryl a place in another school herself. *'I rang around and around until I got her in ... For weeks I didn't get any reply. But one morning ... they got back to me ... and Cheryl started the following day'*. Sheila thought that the most significant impact of exclusion on her child was that she missed her friends at school. *'She was like "can't you try and get me back in there, mum?" and I phoned and they said "no way" and, erm, I phoned again and they were like "no way" and I thought "okay"'*.

Joan felt that she and her son had no support after his exclusion:

> *'We had no support from the school, no support. 'Cos they're supposed to contact the behavioural services, and they're supposed to come in and see what he's like. But we never had none of that. Nothing at all, just nothing. We had the educational bloke down, but I think instead they should have contacted the behavioural support'*.

Joan did not really know what support she could call on: *'I never knew at the time. There was no support there, so I didn't know what I was entitled to'*. Joan was angry about the way her son was treated:

'I'd just had enough! Everything he'd done. I mean, it don't matter what he did. If you read [the school record] it's stupid. He don't hit no teachers or, you know, nothing bad. I mean, that fight was after school. I mean, they're kids, aren't they? I've seen worse than what he's done'.

She added that after exclusion it was several months before Jeremy got a place in a BSC. *'He wasn't at school from February to September ... he had nothing, nothing at all'*. On the impact of exclusion on Jeremy, Joan stated that *'he's lost a lot of time. It's gonna be hard to get back into it'*. In terms of her own day-to-day life, Joan felt that Jeremy's exclusion had affected her ability to get a better job (she worked as a dinner-lady for about an hour-a-day). *'I wanted to get a job but I can't. I think I feel stuck. All it is is meetings and meetings, and plus he's a minor so he's got to be looked after anyway'*. Joan was concerned about the longer-term impact of exclusion on Jeremy's prospects.

Jim and his wife had spent a lot of time liaising with other agencies in seeking support for their daughter and themselves after the exclusion:

'We were hoping for some counselling, some professional advice on why she's behaving like this. Maybe put us under the microscope as well, and our relationship and all the rest of that. To come out the other side with some answers'.

Nina stated that during Nancy's five-months' exclusion she was given no work to do by the school:

'When she was out in February until the end of June, there was no contact. They didn't contact me once, and no work was sent for her. I mean, they said work would be sent to her. But they don't care'.

She also felt that the school did not want to give Nancy a second chance after she returned:

'I don't think their attitude had changed. I don't think they'd changed at all when she went back to school. I think they were looking to throw her out 'cos the headmaster told me that they thought it was best if she found an alternative school. No, I don't think they supported her'.

Nina thought that the main impact of exclusion on her daughter was boredom. She was less concerned about the time she missed out on her education because *'she is bright. She's a quick learner and she can catch up on it all'*.

Perceptions on the effectiveness of exclusion

While Grace did not think that exclusion was an effective way of making pupils change their behaviour she wasn't sure what else schools could ultimately do. She did feel *'a need for more training for teachers to manage disruptive pupils. This should be part of teacher training courses'*. Winnie also felt that excluding 'disruptive' pupils was not an effective way of changing behaviour, adding that it would be preferable to *'give them something to do'*. Sheila thought that a better way of tackling 'disruptive' pupils was to offer better support:

'I think to deal with kids really you need support from parents and from teachers. Really sit down and discuss what are the problems and try and solve the problems together - not just exclude them and think, "well, that's a bad bunch" ... I've another daughter who has been through it, and had no support whatsoever. Now she's 20 she feels no one cares and no one tried to help ... And other kids must be feeling that, and that's why there must be support at home as well for the parents, as well as the school and the family to get together'.

Diane thought that excluding pupils *'has its good side in the fact that you're taking the naughty children away and they're not disrupting the others. But the bad side is then that that child is losing out on education and it's not benefiting him at all, is it?'* Instead, Diane thought:

'maybe they could have a special unit within the school itself and put all the naughty children together so that they wouldn't be so isolated and they could still communicate with friends and school and so on. Yeah, and maybe getting people in to talk to them; to find out what the problems are 'cos, I mean, I know these children who are naughty – it goes a lot deeper than people realise and if they can get to the root of the problem then maybe they might not be so many naughty children. I mean, by punishing them ... I know they need to be punished if they've been naughty but, er, sometimes punishing them doesn't work, does it?'.

Joan thought that rather than exclude Jeremy the school *'should have put him in a class with the other naughty kids and have one teacher to a smaller class - instead of just throwing them out'*. She felt that a better way of managing pupils with 'difficult' behaviour would be to *'put them in smaller groups in the school itself. You know, keep them away from the other kids so they're not disrupting the other kids'*.

Jim suggested an alternative system to exclusion based on his own workplace experience:

'We have an absentee system at work and there is a point system. To be honest, it is very close to the school exclusion process where, if you're late for one day, you get so many points. Late for another day, you get so many

more points until you reach this level with the points that they take money off you. But the difference was, with the absenteeism scheme, that once you've scored so many points and they've taken, say, a day's money off you, you then start at the beginning again. You see, there is none of that "there is no way of wiping the slate clean" ... If we say three-days exclusion is the penalty, and if we say you've done the three days, there has got to be a point where you say "that's it"'.

Still, Jim hoped that Joanna's exclusion might teach her an important lesson about life:

'At the end of the day I have an outlook on life, if you like, that says when a child grows as a toddler they learn that there are certain things they have to accept within the little community of the family. There are rules and there are people who they have to deal with and, as that child grows, by the time we send them to school we are supposed to have taught them, as parents, right and wrong. And they have to, at that point, realise that they are then going into another community. Erm, a community of school if you like. And they go through the process, and some of the values they learn there are that life is not purely about the individual. It is about working within a community of 30 or 40 within a class. That there are things they are allowed to do, and things they are not allowed to do. It ain't just learning your ABC and basic maths and all the rest of it. It's also about learning how to deal with life 'cos when they come out of school there is a big wide world out there. And there is little control over that ... To me, a lesson that she has to learn is that not everybody out there in that big wide world is going to be fair to her, is going to be decent ... So, I'm glad the teachers are like that in one way 'cos it's preparation for her'.

But Jim did feel that exclusion:

'should only be an absolute last resort ... There's certainly a lot of pressure on schools today to perform that is a negative pressure, if you like, on their relationship with the pupils. There is a pressure to perform with the league tables and pressures to perform financially. Those two alone mean schools maybe haven't got enough time for the problem children. They concentrate on getting them out of the way – "let's get the good ones in, 'cos it will boost our school at the end of the year"'.

Instead of excluding Nancy, Nina thought that the school:

'could have helped her on a personal level. More, you know, try and talk to her. But at the end of the day she is very troubled and ... they just didn't wanna know her. So, erm, I just think if they'd have tried a bit harder - I mean, I've said this to the teachers and they've just said "well, where do you draw the line"'.

Perceptions on the City's Behaviour Support Service

Grace felt that the BSC that Glen had attended had benefited her son by getting him back into a routine. She also thought that the use of privileges as an enticement along with help with his anger management had encouraged him to work and behave better. Jenny felt that the BSC Jack eventually attended gave a bad impression to her other two sons because it appeared to reward bad behaviour (for example, they go caving and rock climbing, and have no homework). Winnie described the BSC William attended as *'better than nothing'* but felt that it did not provide much of an education. Pupils only attend two hours per day, 10.00 am to 12.15 pm, which meant William got up late and Winnie did not know what he got up to in the afternoons. Sheila did not think that a BSC would have been suitable for her daughter. She wanted her back into a mainstream school. Joan did not think that the BSC had benefited her son. *'I just think it's too disruptive and not long enough anyway. He ain't getting no work done'*. Nina felt that the BSC Nancy attended offered insufficient help: *'She was only there three days and they kicked her out. I don't think they give her the chance. I don't think they actually sat down and had a one-to-one with her, not in three days. She was only there two hours [a day]. I don't think they tried'*.

Perceptions on schools and teachers

Grace described a 'good' teacher as someone *'experienced, a good manager with respect for pupils'*. She described a 'bad' teacher as someone who *'can't control the class, can't make lessons interesting'*. Jenny felt no respect for teachers or schools. She didn't know any 'good' teachers and thought 'bad' teachers were ones who did not listen. She felt that one teacher had humiliated Jack and when she phoned to complain she felt nothing was done about it. Winnie described a 'good' teacher as someone who *'has humour and understanding, and treats pupils with respect'*. She described a 'bad' teacher as someone who *'humiliates'*. Sheila described a 'good' teacher as *'someone who is there, who understands, who listens and who tries to help the children in the class'*. She described a 'bad' teacher as *'someone who doesn't listen'*. Diane described a 'good' teacher as:

> *'one that you could get on with and have a laugh with. They still did their job, but they had an easier approach as opposed to being strict ... To get on the right foot with kids you've got to make them like you to start with. And if you're the type of teacher who is very strict, and doesn't smile, and are a very sergeant-major type, straight away you've put up a barrier between you and the kids. But if you can be easy with them and joke and laugh, and still do your job, then that's the way I think'.*

Diane would gift teachers with a *'sense of humour'*. She did not feel that a teacher had ever picked-on Dave. *'I don't think it's a problem for Dave 'cos I think he can stand up for himself. So if someone picked-on him he just wouldn't be a victim'*. Joan described a 'good' teacher as *'someone who can listen, is understanding'*. She described a 'bad' teacher as *'all the teachers up there. They don't wanna know, do they?'*. Jim appeared reluctant to judge teachers:

> *'I don't hold any blame in the direction of the teachers. I know they're not perfect. I know there's good and bad in that community of teachers as there is in any, whether it's the workplace or the people you live next door to. I mean, nobody is ever going to be perfect. I would blame the system rather than the individuals. The disciplinary system if you like and the whole education system of pressure to achieve end of year results. I think they are all wrong rather than individual teachers'.*

Nina described a 'good' teacher as someone who has *'got control in the classroom, that can captivate the children, cares about them and is interested in them. Someone who can be there if they have got a problem and can listen to them'*. She described a 'bad' teacher as someone who *'lacks interest'*. Grace said that the thing she would most like to change about schools is *'making sure they were well managed and could handle behaviour well'*. She would also get rid of the bad teachers. The thing Winnie would most like to change about schools is *'no expulsions'*. The thing she would most like to change about teachers is training them to *'treat pupils well'*. What Sheila would most like to change about schools is *'the system in general. The whole system needs to be shaken up and changed'*. Similarly, Joan would like to change *'everything. Throw them [the teachers] all out, start again'*. Nina would most like to see the introduction of an effective students' council. *'I think they should have something like they have in colleges - like a students' council - so that if the children have problems and they can't talk to the teacher (say bullying or problems like that) they can talk to the students' council'*. She would also like to see teachers demonstrate *'more understanding, and to see that pupils are just average kids. Every child is lacking somewhere. Teachers just need to try and be more understanding'*.

Grace was aware of the school rules and agreed that they were 'sensible' rules - covering such things as no swearing, respecting others, wearing the school uniform, being at class on time and not going to the toilet during lessons. She also felt that she had had an opportunity to have a say in how the school was run, but that she had to push for this. Jenny also felt the rules of the school were fair. She did not feel, however, that she had had an opportunity to participate effectively in decisions made about her son's schooling. Winnie said the school never explained to her what the school rules were, and feels that parents/carers do not always have an opportunity to be involved in decisions made about their child's education. While she felt that some schools include parents in decision-making, she thought that William's had not. She felt that she had no power and that the school had all the power, adding *'if I smacked or neglected my son the authorities would take him away; if school smacks or neglects William then they get away with it'*. Joan was aware of the school rules and thought these sensible, but she did not feel that parents/carers had a real opportunity to participate in decisions made about a child's education and did not feel the school really listens. Nina understood the school rules and had no problems with these. She believed them to be sensible. But she did not believe that parents/carers have a genuine opportunity to be involved in decisions made about their child's education. She acknowledged, however, that perhaps she could have done more to be involved. *'I mean, I never have been involved with the school, unless we had a problem. If there was a problem they'd contact me. But if I was more involved with the school there'd be more opportunities to be an influence there'.*

Perceptions on neighbourhood

Grace was generally happy in the neighbourhood she lived, particularly because of local shops and amenities. The thing she disliked most about the area was the number of houses being sold for student accommodation, which was leading to an increase in noisy parties. Jenny liked her neighbours but disliked the drug-dealers/-users in the area: *'they're everywhere you go. You have to put up with it. Ideally, I'd like a 3-bedroomed house in a decent area, but that's not gonna happen'.* Winnie liked where she lived and felt happy there; it was *'quiet'.* She disliked the gangs and people revving up cars. She thought that there could be more useful and positive activities in the area for young people, such as *'building cars'.* Sheila liked the neighbourhood she lived in because it was quiet. She did not express any negative views about it. Joan was not that settled in her neighbourhood:

'It's OK, but since the [Housing Action] Trust took over they just cater for the old people and nothing for the young. And then you have that 'zero tolerance' [to anti-social behaviour] and threatening to evict you. It has got really bad on here, really. If the kids play up they threaten to evict you. Yeah, it's only since they started building all these buildings up, and all the kids are going on them and they're building houses everywhere. There's no room nowhere. There's no parks, no nothing - is there? They've took them all down'.

She would like to see a centre for young people provided. Jim thought there was not a lot for young people to do on his estate. He added, however:

'we're not a million miles away from the city centre. You've also got the local shopping centre nearby and there are youth clubs around there. And there's certainly cinemas around, bowling alleys within certainly a short bus ride ... I don't think it's a case that there has to be facilities right next door'.

He also stated that he felt happy where he lived. Nina liked the neighbourhood she lived in, and could not think of any 'bad' things about it. The only improvement she could suggest was *'just have a centre for the young'.*

Future aspirations

Grace's aspiration for her son was for him to be *'self-sufficient and happy'* in the future. With a push she believed he could be. In respect of Jack's future, Jenny stated:

> *'I don't want him to leave home. No, ideally I'd like to move back to Ireland eventually and let him grow up to be a man over there 'cos I know there's not much he can do wrong over there. He loves it over there. He gets more freedom over there than he gets over here. But if it comes to it, and we've got to stay here, as long as he gets a job. It doesn't have to be a brilliant job as long as he's got money in his pocket and he's safe. That's all that counts'.*

Winnie shares her son's ambition and wants for him a *'good life with dignity'*. She believes he will achieve this. In respect of her daughter's future, Sheila stated *'what I want and what she wants are two different things. But I would like her to travel the world and believe she will because she's determined'*. Diane hoped Dave would go on to study at college, and acknowledged that he may go abroad to work:

> *'I would prefer him though, before he does go abroad, to get some sort of, erm, trade or something behind him for future reference. Whether he uses it or not for the time being is neither here nor there. But if anything falls through abroad, you never know what's gonna happen, you've always got something to fall back on. And I'd prefer it, and I will do my best to make sure he does do something like that, before he does toddle off ... He's got the intelligence, and he's certainly got the personality. He can go places if he channels it all in the right direction and uses his loaf. He can go places. I've already told him that. He is a good lad. He is a good lad.'*

Joan would like to see her son achieve his ambition of joining the army, but fears that his educational experience may prove to be a barrier. Jim would like to see Joanna succeed in the future in some area of performing art:

> *'She certainly has an aptitude for anything physical - her dancing, gymnastics, trampolining, anything like that. She's very good at dancing in particular, so I think she's going to go, I hope for her sake, into some form of performing arts or some kind of thing'.*

While Joanna had mentioned the possibility of going on to college or university, Jim stated that:

> *'I can't see her doing it. I would like it. But I'm struggling with that one I'm afraid. I'm sorry, it's a bit unfair I suppose for a parent to sit here and say "well, I would like to see her go to university" when, if what she's really*

interested in is getting out in the world and, I don't know, becoming a pop star. So it's a bit of a waste of time her going to college'.

In respect of Nancy's future, Nina stated that *'I hope that she gets a good job with a reasonable salary, and that she hasn't really got to struggle. I'd like her to be comfortable'.* When asked if she thought Nancy would achieve this, Nina replied *'yes, I think she will'.*

Key issues raised

Similar to the pupil respondents, most parents/carers felt their child's exclusion was unjust and that, on the whole, had been for minor incidents or unsubstantiated. Only Jim stated that it was fair, although in Joanna's case he did feel preventative action might have avoided the necessity of exclusion. Most parent/carer respondents expressed resentment about the school system: that their child had been picked-on and treated disrespectfully, and that insufficient support had been offered in respect of anger management or learning difficulties. Jim thought that the planned financial penalties on schools that excluded had encouraged his daughter's (and other's) exclusion prior to their introduction.

Parent/carer respondents' experiences of the exclusion process were largely negative. On the whole they believed, as did the pupils, that schools and governors were unresponsive to their needs. In particular, parents/carers felt that they did not have access to effective advice and support during and after the exclusion process, leaving them with feelings of abandonment and stress. Jim described the process as a 'runaway train' – once it had started there seemed no way of reversing it. Most of the respondents confirmed the profound negative feelings expressed by the pupils about the effects of their exclusion: isolation; low self-esteem; depression; stigma; fear; confusion; distress. A number of respondents also shared some of these feelings themselves. Most of the respondents shared the pupils' view that exclusion is not an effective way of changing behaviour. Similar alternatives to exclusion were also suggested: better support (such as counselling); in-school centres; smaller classes; more practical activities. Grace added that she felt teacher training needed to give more emphasis to managing disruptive pupils. Jim added that exclusion has taught his daughter that the real world is not necessarily a fair place, a 'valuable' preparation for life.

Parents/carers were less positive than their children about the special provision received from BSCs. The main reason for this was the very short days. Parents/carers felt that their children were doing insufficient schoolwork and were concerned about what they got up to the rest of the day. Grace was more positive about the BSC her son attended, believing it had given him back a routine and helped deal with his anger.

Defining a 'good' teacher, parent/carer respondents highlighted many of the attributes identified by the pupils: humorous; respectful; good classroom management skills; empathetic and caring; good listening skills; fair; captivating. Similarly a 'bad' teacher: lacks interest; poor classroom management skills; does not listen; disrespectful. What parent/carer respondents most wanted to change about school included: better classroom management; the removal of 'bad' teachers; the abolition of expulsions; training teachers to respect. Nina wanted to see the introduction of more effective pupil support through the school council. Most parents/carers thought that their child's school rules were sensible, but there was mixed feeling about the extent of parent/carer involvement in decisions made about how the school was run.

As with the pupil respondents, parents/carers generally expressed positive experiences about their neighbourhood. But again, some concerns were also highlighted including a lack of facilities for young people, drugs and gangs. Joan also raised concerns about New Labour's 'zero tolerance' policies against so-called 'anti-social behaviour', including the threat of eviction. Finally, parent/carer respondents largely shared their children's aspirations for the future, with some also sharing their concerns that exclusion from school could prove a barrier to achievement.

Chapter five

The perceptions of teachers

Experiences of permanent exclusion

Mr PH had had little recent experience of exclusion because his present school adopted a policy of not to exclude.

In Mr RR's school the main reasons for exclusions have included assaults on teachers and fights between pupils. Mr RR felt that some of these might have been avoided.

Ms PM stated that her school had experienced relatively few disciplinary problems, adding:

> *'the pupils here feel very well supported. They are very proud of their school. I think also, of course, in this area the family structure is still quite strong. And in Years 10,11,12 and 13 most children still have two parents who care about them, and who care about their education and are prepared to intervene should something go wrong. Lower down the school we are noticing an increase in instances of poor behaviour, and this is presumably coming as the kids become increasingly "westernised" and fight against the structures of the family'.*

The popularity of Ms PM's school is evidenced in the demand for places: *'we always have a waiting list. I mean, I've got a waiting list of 63 in Year 10'* – which allows the school to select pupils who *'fit in'.* Ms PM stated that:

> *'the last person to be permanently excluded was on the 30 June 1998 and that was a Year 9 boy who I never knew. Since amalgamation in 1993 we have probably only had about five pupils permanently excluded. We do everything in our power to keep them here, much to the staff's, er ... well, you can imagine it!'.*

The school has used temporary exclusions more where pupils are excluded for two or three days. Ms PM had experienced excluded pupils coming to her school:

> *'We are quite surprised because, very often, they are very well behaved ... Generally, they don't seem the sort of child who would be excluded, you know what I mean? Personality wise. I can think of one boy who was excluded from another local school for allegedly throwing a stone at a teacher. Now, this child was very, very quiet, you know. He never said "boo" to a goose'.*

Ms CC stated that about 2 pupils had been excluded from her school over the last two years. *'One of them in particular - she was just completely out of control, completely and utterly out of control. I mean, she was given loads of warnings etc. and eventually she assaulted the head'.* Ms CC did not think that these exclusions were avoidable. Prior to exclusion pupils are counselled regularly and warned as to the consequences of their behaviour - both verbally and in writing - so when exclusion happens *'it's not a shock for them at all'.*

Ms BG's school had had no exclusions in the previous two years. She added:

'I don't think we could say that that is a mark of the great success of our policies and practices alone. It's partly related to the nature of the intake [mainly Pakistani girls], that this is a school where the children who come are, by and large, extremely positive about education, and this may be to do with the background that they come from. They are often youngsters who do expect to follow the rules, so many of the issues that arise in a school, especially inner-city schools, don't arise in the same way here. I think it's connected [to culture]. I think there is a correlation ... Nationally and locally, Pakistani girls' exclusion rates are extremely low and, given that our population is almost entirely girls of Pakistani heritage, one might expect that the exclusion rate would be low here I think'.

Mr KM stated that exclusions at his school had been for *'all kinds of reasons. Violence, racial abuse, swearing'.* He added:

'In the main we [now] use exclusions as a last possible resort. If somebody's excluded permanently it's normally because they've gone through a number of stages and, at the final stage, they are told if this kind of behaviour continues then they will be excluded. There's normally a process that we go through, unless it's something like severe violence to somebody - a teacher or something like that - it may warrant a fixed-term'.

Mr IB's experience of exclusion at his school had been largely affected by the appointment of a new head teacher:

'we have a new head teacher who started in March, and she wants to sort of try and stamp on poor behaviour. The last head was very strong on discipline, and there was a danger that the new head - er, it was the first woman head the school has had - might be perceived as a bit of a softie. So she said "zero tolerance" on certain types of behaviour'.

In terms of exclusions over the previous two years Mr IB was not certain. *'I would guess about ten, but I'm guessing'.* Mr IB did not think that these exclusions could have been avoided given *'the current climate of education - its funding and that'.*

Ms MD's school had excluded 9 pupils over the previous two years. Exclusions were due to mainly physical abuse to other students and *'defiance of school rules, like not responding to authority and that'*. Ms MD thought that *'given time, staff and energy, you could avoid most of them'*.

Perceptions on the causes of 'challenging' behaviour

Mr PH thought the fundamental causes of 'challenging' behaviour reflected a complex mix of factors. These include the pupil's:

'own background and social patterns established at home and their approach to solving problems; ...a sense of injustice ... resentment ... no matter how dishonest that might be; ... frustration at being unable to cope [because] the work may be too difficult for them; ... peer group relationships [and] experimentation with drugs'.

These factors may be exacerbated by:

'insensitive or poor teaching at times ... Some teachers expect standards of pupils which they don't achieve themselves ... We can be extremely rude at times, yet expect pupils to be polite to us. We are in an empowered position and power is often quite insidious. It's difficult to avoid abusing it because you often don't realise how you are abusing it. And this hinges on this sense of injustice that drives some kids wild'.

Mr PH also raised concerns about constraints imposed by the National Curriculum on pupils' behaviour, referring to the danger of turning a child into a *'commodity ... stuffed and packaged and set out into the world ... instead of looking at the child from the child's needs'*. He called for more meaningful assessments, *'testing for success rather than "catching" pupils out'*.

Mr RR thought that the main causes of 'challenging' behaviour were linked to 'home' and 'hormones':

'When they become teenagers they become a "Kevin". It's also trouble within the family, the break-up of the family and even to physical and sexual abuse. In some cases it can be due to poor teacher-pupil relationships, or external influences such as drugs on the street, growing violence in society - it's a jungle out there sometimes - or police attitudes to young people'.

Mr RR, however, also saw the regulatory framework for education as part of the problem:

'At the end of the day you are results driven - we are pushing, pushing, pushing for the improvement of exam results. And we get the improvement of exam results, but penalise the certain pupils who don't fit in easily with the system'.

He felt that all the extra work expected of schools was causing a strain on teachers and that *'this must impact on teacher-pupil relationships and behaviour in the classroom'*.

Part of the problem, suggested Ms PM, was parental control:

'A lot of these parents, they wouldn't have enough control over their children, certainly as they get older, to ensure that they do something sensible, do you know what I mean? Particularly the boys ... Er, the boys seem to be able to do almost what they want'.

Ms CC thought the fundamental cause of 'challenging' behaviour was due to the pupil *'not placing a value on education, not seeing the long-term effects of it I think. This probably comes from the home and also just disaffection generally. They see themselves as apart from society almost'*. Ms CC also thought that some excluded pupils might have learning difficulties.

Ms BG felt that the fundamental cause of 'challenging' behaviour is *'not succeeding ... If you don't succeed, what's the point? "Just fail me". Feeling that you're not succeeding, feeling that you're not part of it'*.

Mr KM suggested various aspects to the causes of 'challenging' behaviour:

'I think there are several strands ... The strand at home where it may be that there is no role model at home or, from their point of view, standards are not maintained for whatever reason, that they carry a lot of baggage from home that they bring into school. For example, from the social disadvantage side of things, you know that they're not cared for, or there might be family problems. The stability within the family home isn't there, and that impacts, that makes them insecure and there's an element of that instability that comes into school ... And there's, within school, erm, the fact that perhaps there is not a clearly defined standard of behaviour, where the pupil may be confused over what is acceptable and what isn't. It may be because a pupil is not liked, erm. I'm not saying that happens here, but just talking in general terms as to why a pupil might misbehave. It may be that they find the work too easy and they want someone to stimulate them; or the work is too difficult and they want more support. Er, you know, there's a range of things that make a pupil misbehave'.

Mr IB thought that the causes of difficult behaviour were *'fundamentally ... a matter of social skills that have not developed at an early enough age. I would see, probably, that those lack of social skills are caused by, erm, I don't know - socio-economic deprivation, etc.'*. In addition to this, however, Mr IB saw the context within which teachers teach as a contributory factor:

'I really think that the pressures that teachers are put under is a contributory factor - not a fundamental factor, but certainly a contributory factor because we are judged on so much. You know, we've got threshold performances where my salary or whether I can get this extra money is going to be judged on whether I can prove that not only do my class do well but that they did better than other classes. And if I've got, you know, real pressure on to get results, because that's what we are going to be judged on, and virtually that's it now, that has implications for what happens in your lower sets. We have a tremendous teacher shortage crisis at the moment so, what are we doing? Putting all our decent teachers in the top sets and all our supply teachers in the bottom sets. Supply teachers can't control [and] one of the reasons these students are misbehaving is because they are seeing a different teacher every week, every day at some stages now. That does not help the students'.

Mr IB outlined the sorts of pressure teachers were under:

'Firstly, you've got the pressure of OFSTED; secondly, you've got the pressure of being judged by a national standard - you are not judged by your situation, which we find appalling. You saw the building works when you came in. I mean, what it's like working around this! I mean, this has been going on for years. We've built this building, that building, the other building ... But OFSTED will not take that into account at all ... It doesn't say "this poor bloke's there, doing his best ... they've got building problems". It says, "not only have they got all these other problems, they also have this problem too". Erm, we're judged on our A-Cs. Our A-Gs at this school are fantastic. We get better A-Gs than in this so called "wonderful school" up the road, but we're not really judged on A-Gs ... You're not judged on what else you've contributed to the students. You're not judged on "value-added". So we have all the judgments made on us - as professionals – that are horrifically bias against us. And that means that you end up feeling I'm going to have to slog my guts out to overcome all that. Now I happen to think that's why they do it - because they think a lot of us are lazy and they actually want to put threats over our heads ... They're saying they want to raise standards but they aren't ...The other thing which is more on going is the teacher shortage. Last week we were nine teachers short ... 20 per cent of our workforce out of action for one reason or another ... So the teacher shortages make things very difficult'.

Ms MD thought that 'challenging' behaviour reflected family factors and the inability of schools to respond flexibly to these:

'I think some of our students come with a lot of baggage. They've got a lot of dysfunctional families. We've got a lot of families who are in financial difficulties; we've got families who are in trouble with the law; we've got families who, you know, with dependency problems - alcohol, drugs. So

we've got a lot of children who have got very difficult backgrounds, who find it very difficult to socialise ... We've got a number of students now which we are forced to include in our school who I think should have been provided for in a different way because there are very few sort of units now for children who need small provision ... And I personally think that we need a great deal more support with, er, students with, you know, special educational needs. Our staff need more training on how to deal with them, er, and I think that schools haven't got the flexibility to deal with a lot of the problems that are coming into school now'.

Perceptions on tackling 'challenging' behaviour

Mr PH saw the need for a collective approach to tackling 'challenging' behaviour that used *'the strengths of those teachers who can provide the necessary structures in their own class. They can go in as a "support teacher" if you like and assist with a difficult group'.* Mr RR did not believe that teacher training offered teachers the necessary tools to manage challenging behaviour. *'You actually learn how to manage challenging behaviour on the job ... It's largely about building relationships'.* Neither did Mr RR feel that schools had the resources to tackle the causes of 'challenging' behaviour. In particular teachers lacked:

'time ... we don't have the time to sit for hours and talk to children who need our help because we are under pressure to improve our assessment and exam results, or to complete our performance pay application form. They reward teachers who have demonstrated the ability to write something coherent on 8 pages of an application form ... They don't see the relationship teachers have with the kids. The pieces of paper I have had to fill in so that somebody else can judge if I'm worthy of my salary! It's getting a bit out of hand!'

In contrast, Ms PM felt her school did have the resources to tackle 'challenging' behaviour, *'bearing in mind that here the behaviour isn't very dysfunctional. I mean, half of our staff would say that our children are awfully behaved. But they're not'.* The school has internal training in behaviour management, including some provided by the new behaviour support worker:

'Things are explained to them [the teachers], the strategies they can use. But half the staff don't use them. All they do is pass it over to me [as head] if a child is badly behaved ... I know they [some teachers] want them kicked out. But, I mean, they haven't really done anything'.

Ms CC did not feel her school had the resources to tackle 'challenging' behaviour, adding that *'I don't think anyone has'.* She believed there is a need for *'smaller classes in a particular unit where some of them could be helped and supported maybe'* and *'more money, more teachers'*. She did not feel that teacher training provided the necessary tools to manage behaviour.

Ms BG also questioned whether schools had the necessary resources to tackle 'challenging' behaviour and felt that more money and expertise were needed:

> *'The type of expertise that would be particularly useful here in this school would be things that give children access to out-of-hours enrichment activities ... [such as] after-school classes to offer accelerated exam entry, ... rock climbing, going away for weekends, ...[and] summer university camps'.*

Ms BG expressed more optimism about teacher training providing some of the tools for managing behaviour. *'I think the students that you see coming in from teacher training colleges are, by and large, super and have much stronger training than ... we saw coming in before. So I think there is a much more focused approach to managing pupil behaviour'.* In contrast Ms BG believed that:

> *'the notion of INSET, equated with going out on a course for the day, clearly doesn't help and we use that infrequently for anything to do with managing a classroom or managing behaviour. I'd much rather save my pennies and buy someone in to come and work here with a group of people and at the place where it's happening'.*

Mr KM did not believe that schools had the necessary resources to manage 'challenging' behaviour, particularly *'the staffing expertise to deal with these pupils'*. He felt that schools had yet to develop effective structures to ensure that pupils displaying 'challenging' behaviour remained integrated within the mainstream:

> *'In the old days you used to send a child to a centre. Erm, I'm not saying if that was right or that was wrong, but there was an element of real support there for the child. The structure in school isn't quite right yet in my opinion. There is a need, erm, not necessarily to staff these centres with teachers, but to staff them with other expertise ... Certainly one-to-one counselling, certainly patience, certainly the ability to tackle children who have faced abuse, and psychological expertise to get behind the veneer and that. I think teachers are not skilled to do that'.*

Mr IB did not think that schools had the necessary resources to tackle 'challenging' behaviour. *'My fundamental thing is class size. I don't care what OFSTED say, if you have 30 kids in a class you're struggling to cope'.* Neither did he think that teacher training was providing the necessary tools to manage behaviour:

'I've been here ten years and have a lot of experience ... In my opinion almost everything I see on behaviour management is Titanic stuff, you know ... As an example, we had a new teacher who was a supply teacher that had a difficult class so someone who had been on behaviour management training said "I will come and help you". I said, "oh, can I sit in?" (since she was in my department). So, she came in and said things like "there's not much display on the walls, that's not a very good teaching arrangement". If she thinks she's going to stick some display on the walls and rearrange the chairs, and the class are going to start behaving, she's living in cloud-cuckoo-land!'.

Ms MD did not think that schools had the resources to tackle 'challenging' behaviour:

No, and I don't think there is support for it. I mean, things like education psychology. I mean, they're not miracle workers, but we only see one for a morning, once a half term. I mean, that's not enough. We've got a very good pupil in-school support - comes in one morning a week, you know. That's good. We've got a brilliant ESW. But yet we have to pay for behaviour support, which is quite expensive. Things like anger management groups, socialising groups, you know ... You need that kind of support ... And I really don't think that there is enough support ... I'm all for inclusion, erm, and I think that as many children as possible should be in mainstream school. But I think that the inclusion programme has been at a detriment to a lot of students. There's a lot them been thrust into school having not been offered the specialist support that they need. I mean, you know you've got a student on retrolin and ABHD and you've got all of these things and really, how do you deal with a student like that because I haven't got any training in that? We're having training in dealing with partially-sighted children and things like that. But you know, at the end of the day, we've got thirty-odd students in a class, you know. You need some extra assistance yourself for the other children'.

Ms MD did not think that in-service training helped much:

'I don't think there's enough time to do it. I mean, you know, you look at the INSET days we've had this year. You know performance management systems to be part of that, and then you've got all the other things. And these kinds of things [behaviour management training] tend to get put on the back burner. But they are very important'.

Perceptions on the exclusion process

At Ms CC's school 'disruptive' pupils would be counselled regularly prior to exclusion, presented with targets and warned as to the consequences of their behaviour. *'So that when exclusion happens it's not a shock for them at all'.*

Once excluded support for the child and/or parent/carer usually came from educational social workers (ESWs), although Ms CC stated that it was usually up to the parent/carer to arrange this.

Mr KM believed that most schools in the City were now seeking to avoid exclusions as a strategy:

'we've got in-house provision, what we call our "time-out workgroup", which is an alternative to exclusion. So some exclusions wouldn't be excluded now ... They would go into the workgroup for a fixed period of time. So the actual structure within the school has very much changed somewhat than it was perhaps two or three years ago ... Three or four years ago we had a very high level of exclusions. Erm, naturally it's still high, but it has come down appreciably in the last two to three years ...

Mr KM believed that parents and pupils were involved at every stage of the process:

'We have a full head teacher disciplinary which is at the end of the process where the parents will come in. We'll have an interview and we'll say to them that we'll go through the process. We'll set targets knowing that if they do fall by the wayside of that then they've had a chance. But parents are involved at every step of the way'.

Mr IB stated that his school would consult with the pupil and parent/carer prior to the threat of permanent exclusion:

'Whenever somebody returns from [temporary] exclusion they have to come in with their parents to talk things over ... and the students are not allowed into any class until it's been thoroughly discussed with parents, guardians or whatever. The parents are told that "these are the behaviours that are acceptable - do you agree they are acceptable?" Contracts are signed by the student: "I will not do such and such at school, etc." If that contract is repeatedly broken, erm, and the education of the rest is repeatedly disrupted then, at that point, to be honest, what we normally do ...is we contact the parents and say "you do realise that there is obviously no way that your child is going to remain in this school - they're on their last chance" ... As long as you can demonstrate you've tried your best then exclusions are more likely to be approved. Under those circumstances, very often, a child will be removed to go to another school before they have the stigma of being permanently excluded. So actually, the number that have been permanently excluded is disguised as those that have been told unofficially - this is the previous head, I can't speak for the new head - unofficially "your child is going to get permanently excluded within 12 months ... they need a new start, they need something fresh"'.

Mr IB did not think, however, that pupils and parents/carers were involved in any ultimate decision to exclude. Once excluded, Mr IB explained, teachers are expected to set and mark work for the pupil:

'*The theoretical position is that ... it is the responsibility of staff to continue to send work and mark that work. Therefore, the form tutor or year tutor will, erm, initially ask for work to be assessed and, if that's not forthcoming, actually send an envelope to each teacher individually and say "put some work in this envelope for me". That envelope is then sent home and we tell them "when that is returned finished we'll get you some more". I personally cannot remember, ever, a student coming back for a second lot of work so we've covered our backs, if you like, in saying "we sent the work, we will send more when that's finished". But our experience is that the students that we have excluded basically wouldn't do work in class – there's no damn way they're going to do it at home. So that's all we've ever done. It's never come back for marking*'.

Mr IB was not aware of any specific support offered to parents/carers of excluded pupils.

In respect of involvement in the decision to exclude, Ms MD stated that pupils were '*involved in the sense that they know a long way back down the line where things are going, and they know that they're in the system and [told] "This is the pattern of your behaviour, this is what happens next"*'. Ms MD argued that parents/carers were involved in the sense that:

'*They're told, "if your child continues, and we don't have a solution, or we don't have a change, then he is going to be permanently excluded". And they will, obviously, have been to the governors before permanent exclusion as well so, erm, I think that they are aware*'.

The support Ms MD's school made available to children after exclusion was provided through a pupil referral unit or BSC:

'*All of ours go through a pupil referral unit ... But I still think it's a lengthy business, and I think it is ad hoc really, how quickly it happens. Some seem to go through very quickly, and they get a place. And then another child doesn't get there for weeks, you know, months sometimes. It all depends on holidays, staffing, etc. whether there is a place at that particular time. So I don't think that it is particularly good*'.

In terms of support for parents, Ms MD stated that:

'*I think that the Exclusion Team in the City, the ladies who run that team, are very good at supporting parents when they ring up, you know. They are there to help with what you're concerned about, what's happening, and they do give good advice. And they are always there, and they will always deal with parents who want to know things, you know. They do have very sympathetic ears. Whether that's the kind of support that parents really need, I mean, I think at that time parents really want to move on and get their kid into the next stage of school'.*

Perceptions on the impact of permanent exclusion on the child

Mr PH stated that he felt the impact of exclusion on the child:

'must be desperate ... terrible ... I think of my own child and think "how would you like your own child treated like that". That sort of exclusion excludes them from everything ... a sense of belonging, partnership, tolerance, understanding, awareness of other people's needs as well as their own needs ... A child needs approval and a sense of significance ... There's no way they are going to divorce that exclusion from their own personal view of the way others see them ... If we believe in what we are doing in schools, in terms of creating a better life for these pupils, if we exclude them from that then we are, by definition, creating a worse one'.

Mr RR also thought that the impact of exclusion on a child must be *'devastating ... It reinforces the attitude that you're a failure'.* Ms PM also believed that the effects of exclusion would be very damaging:

'There are very few pupils who actually warrant permanent exclusion. You know, they haven't really done anything so bad. If they are permanently excluded their future lies in maybe an hour, or two hours a day if they are lucky, at some centre. Erm, so, they are free for an awful lot of the day, aren't they. There's no structure really, and I think these sorts of kids particularly, and presumably any child really with an awful lot of free time, become bored and get involved in crime and drugs'.

Ms CC was less pessimistic:

'I honestly, firmly believe that they can have a second chance elsewhere. I think if they have really messed up in one place, you know, for different reasons and so on, I really do feel genuinely that they've got to make a fresh start somewhere else ... In this City there's a marvellous centre called the Imani Centre ... I used to work with Ms MH who runs it and she was very, very good ... She does a good job with them because she has a few at a time ... she always had this rapport with the children ... My own feeling is they should have a fresh start elsewhere, I really do. And it will do them good'.

Ms BG thought that the impact of exclusion would be variable:

'depending on whether the exclusion was unusual for that pupil or whether it was something that, in view of all the other indicators, might have been

easily and readily predicted. So I think the impact of exclusion is probably in proportion to the degree of shock that it brings with it'.

Mr KM's response to the effects of exclusion focused on the group of pupils as a whole:

'Ultimately ... what you have to realise in all this process is that it's the learning and the safety of all the pupils in the teaching group or the school that is paramount. So, erm, it's just getting that balance right because you've then got the parents who are expecting a certain standard of behaviour within the school, erm, fearing that, if there's an element of violent behaviour or an element of persistent misbehaviour in the classroom, their child's education is suffering'.

Mr IB thought that the effect of exclusion would depend on the type of child:

'I can see two types. I can see the type ... who says "I can't be bothered" or even "I could be bothered, but look what happened - so therefore, why should I try any harder". But I have also personal experience of kids who come into my class, excluded from other schools, to have a fresh start and who are almost trapped in their behaviour, like peer pressure. There's a kid in this school who I know, one-to-one, I can have a good chat with. He's fine. But somehow, in front of the class, he feels if I behaved in that lesson, sir, they'd all laugh at me. They'd say, "what's up with you today, David?" He feels completely trapped in that behaviour. Now if he's put into another school where they don't know him, he'd get a fresh start. And we have some tremendous success stories at this school of students who were excluded elsewhere, came here with all sorts of background problems, pulled through and got good GCSEs ... So I can see that it can be a very positive benefit. But it depends on the circumstances. I do also see other people - I have experience on the church side – alternative ones, ones who now have court proceedings pending against them'.

Ms MD also thought that the impact of exclusion would depend on the child:

'I think that varies quite a bit. I think for some of them it's a good thing because they pull themselves together, er. Sometimes they manage to get the kind of support they need that they perhaps couldn't get here, although it is increasingly difficult to get into special schools or special units or smaller units, erm, or behaviour support. Sometimes it's a jolt and a fresh start that they need ... We do occasionally get pupils who write back and say, "I've started a new school, and it's going well". And for some, I think, it is the end of the road. I think for one or two of them the school is sometimes the only stability they have, and once they lose that they just go down a slippery slope and get into trouble with the police ... So for some of them it's devastating'.

Perceptions on the impact of permanent exclusion on the parent/carer

Mr PH saw two main possibilities for the way exclusion impacted upon the parent/carer, depending upon relationships at home. For some it could just *'confirm what they thought of their child'*. For others *'it could create a shared sense of resentment against society and those with the power'*. Either way there can be *'nothing positive from it'*. Mr RR did not feel that exclusion impacted on parents/carers. Ms PM thought the impact would depend on the parent/carer:

'If it was somebody who didn't care, you know, it wouldn't have much impact. Some, I imagine, would be very angry and, er, possibly would vent it on the school. Others, I imagine, would just not know what to do. More switched-on parents would know what to do and ring the schools to get them in'.

Ms CC thought that the impact could be problematic:

'I would think [it would cause] quite an anxious time really. Quite difficult because, of course, schools are there with league tables and so on, and are not very anxious to take children back or take a new one that we know the history of. And if you have too many in the same school then it's very, very difficult. So parents are very worried in case they don't get back in'.

Ms BG believed that the impact would be:

'extremely variable. One of the reasons for particularly wanting to avoid exclusion in this particular school would be that it would be absolutely lovely [for some pupils] because being excluded would mean actually being at home with all the nice things that they might associate that with (holidays etc.). It wouldn't be a punishment for those youngsters. And while their parents might well be shocked and very disappointed in their daughters for having been excluded, I think the mothers of those ... children ... would probably actually welcome the extra pair of hands as well. So it wouldn't be a huge hardship for those particular girls. Now that's talking about three particular children who I know ... I think it is particularly difficult for carers to do what schools would sometimes hope they will do - which is make life miserable for the child who is excluded in order that he or she won't want to be excluded again because ... with all the best will in the world ... it is extremely difficult to sustain that. And I defy most of us to manage it with our own youngsters'.

Mr KM thought that the impact of exclusion:

'from the parents' point of view is something they find, erm, they don't feel happy with. They feel it like they've been tainted or tarred with the same brush. You know it's, er, something they feel is an indictment on them. They

feel that they've been let down by their child and they feel ashamed ... Being a parent myself, I know how it would impact on me if my child was excluded from school. You take it personally and you're then left with the responsibility, to some degree, of trying to help with the education and development of your child'.

Mr IB imagined that parents/carers *'go through a range of emotions. I imagine at times it's, erm, "I failed my child". I imagine at times it's "my child has failed me". I imagine at times it's "the system has failed me". I imagine at times it's "that school has failed me"'.* Ms MD also imagined different reactions:

'I think sometimes that parents realise that the school has got to the end of the road ... I think that some parents, you know, realise that the school has done everything and it's just, you know, it's just inevitable really. I think there's some parents who are extremely angry, er, some parents who feel that it's unfair, erm, and that their kids have been slung out ... and so they're very bitter about it, erm. And I think that some parents do feel that they've been let down really and they're floating around and they don't really know very much about it'.

Perceptions on the effectiveness of exclusion

Mr PH did think there might be circumstances when it was necessary to exclude a child:

'You get to the point when you have to balance that one child's needs with the needs of everyone else in the class ... That one child can make it impossible for everyone else ... We can only go so far with the constant bombardment from children who are difficult ... And you have to survive yourself'.

Mr RR did not believe excluding pupils was an effective way of changing their behaviour. Instead, strategies need to respond to the individual pupil's need. *'You've got to look at the individual's character and ... devise a strategy to suit that child. Exclusion is not going to have an effect'.* Ms CC thought excluding a child might have short-term benefits *'but not on its own'.* There is also the need for *'a highly trained teacher and small classes. That's the lack of resources really'.* Ms BG did see a role for excluding pupils: *'I think exclusion is necessary and I would hope and expect that it would be exercised carefully and judicially with a view to particularly considering the immediate health and safety of other pupils and people working in the school'.* She thought that excluding a child may change his or her behaviour, but again it would depend on the degree of shock that exclusion caused. Then again:

'excluding a pupil isn't always done to make a child change their behaviour. Excluding a pupil is done as a breathing space to create a plan so no; I don't think that my experience of exclusion in other settings is to

generally make the pupil change. You do get those infrequent occasions where the shock of the exclusion does work as a strong first step. But I think schools do it to buy space and to consider the plan of how to support and reintegrate the child. I'm sure it won't be perceived like that by the youngsters, unless someone goes through that with them. But I don't know if I would go through that with a child necessarily. I might leave them thinking "it's because you've been naughty"'.

Mr KM thought that the effect of exclusion on a child's behaviour would depend *'on the child because, for some children, it can be just the ticket. For other pupils, for hardened individuals, it may not be. It depends really on the individual case - and that's not a cop out, it's genuinely the case'.* Mr IB did not think that exclusion was an effective way of changing behaviour:

'No, erm I don't … I think the best way is small class sizes because "success breeds success" … If they are a weak student and they were put into a smaller group where they got individual attention then they will be better. I'll give you some examples. I was in with a supply teacher, erm. A kid was going mad – again, he's got special needs. I came in to stop the kids throwing aeroplanes, get them to sit down. Only, this child was running around the classroom. So I say to him, "what do you want to draw?". He said "what? Can you draw?". And I said, "what could you draw on your folder?". I didn't start screaming "sit in you chair!" but "what can you draw on your folder?". So he comes up to look at his folder. "What do you like? Birds? What's the best bird? Draw that". And he's alright, and he's away now. I could do that because the supply teacher was getting the rest of the class started. If he had had 10 kids in that class he could have done it. In fact, he's a damn good teacher … A decent teacher could do that with any child that you've got, so I would like to see that. I don't think it will happen, but that's what I'd like to see'.

Ms MD did not think exclusions changed a child's behaviour:

'I mean, we do use fixed-term as, sometimes, a space, you know, to give them a cooling-off period, to give staff a period where they can look at a student, and put some sort of support in place or whatever. Erm, so does it change their behaviour? On the whole, no, it doesn't change their behaviour. Just being off school doesn't change behaviour. It's what you do when they return, or how the parent is going to change the behaviour. But that's long term'.

Perceptions on New Labour's policies on school inclusion

Mr PH raised a number of concerns about New Labour's policies in relation to dealing with school exclusion:

'Special centres which are appropriate to meet the difficulties of some pupils are being closed down. For whatever the educational excuses given,

these schools are being closed down, it seems to me, for an entirely dishonest economic measure because they are expensive. Yet kids are worth the expense. And they can work in an environment appropriate to their needs ... Current policies of "inclusion" are a cheap trick ... placing pupils in a situation where their needs are not properly addressed and where they feel they are properly cared for, looked after and valued'.

He believed that there was still a need for centres where pupils are *'wanted'*, where they can *'work on a short-term basis ... and have some "time out" for reflection'* and which also offer an in-school support service. Mr PH did feel that some recent initiatives, such as 'Excellence in Cities' and the release of funds for in-school support and mentoring systems, were moves in the right direction. He added, however:

'The concept of "inclusion" is a contradiction in terms. If you are saying that everyone should be in a mainstream school then everyone should be included in an environment that is right for them. If the education system was set up to meet everyone's needs then all pupils would be in the right place of learning. Instead, all pupils have to meet set standards which, for some, may not be meaningful'.

Mr RR did not think that New Labour's current initiatives on school inclusion would work. For instance:

'the government's ideas on mentoring and my ideas on mentoring are two completely different things. I mean, they are banging on about the wonderful idea of having a personal advisor but, if you actually look at the Connexion Service and the person who supplies it, there's going to be one person who devises it for a school like this for 500 children - so there's a lack of personal involvement. He puts someone in who has no experience of working in education to be a mentor ... It's not going to work. It's one of those things that no one has thought through. They come up with ideas but half of them don't work'.

Instead, Mr RR suggested that policy-makers should:

'come and talk to people like me who've been teaching for thirty years. I've worked in a secondary school ... I've worked in a public school ... I've done lots of other things as well ... lots of marketing, PR work ... All kinds of things. I think I've got an idea of what the kids need'.

He went on to say that:

'an awful lot of what we expect is sadly unrealistic. I mean, the pressure is on - in particular assessment results. I know for a fact that it has led to cheating in SATs exams. And nobody's looking at it from the point of view

of the pupil ... There are all these ideas about the GCSEs that are required for industry at the moment. But is it what the pupils want?'

Ms PM stated, under New Labour, finance was now a more significant factor influencing decisions on whether to exclude or not. Under New Labour, schools lose £8000 for each pupil they exclude:

'That's another reason why our head wouldn't exclude unless, really, erm, you know, it had to be done, because it's quite a lot of money. You lose the £8000 and then, when the pupil goes to another school - assuming they go to another school - you lose the £2000 or whatever you get for each pupil that follows the pupil'.

Ms PM was ambivalent about New Labour's stated aim of keeping pupils in school:

'I think for some kids yes. But I still think, probably, in certain schools, there are kids who are either, I don't know, so violent, so disruptive, that keeping them in school just effects the other 1000 pupils. And is that fair? I would say not'.

Ms CC thought that some recent initiatives, such as the introduction of learning mentors, were moves in the right direction. *'We have mentors in the school. I have to say they do make a difference. But I think it depends on the quality of the learning mentor myself'.* Having said this, whether mentors had impacted on behavioural problems was difficult to assess because their focus is on helping with learning difficulties. *'There may be the odd ones that overlap, but in the main it is for those with learning difficulties'.*

Ms BG thought that some New Labour policy objectives were commendable. *'I think it is wise to move towards a policy of social inclusion. I'm hugely in favour of that policy of social inclusion, and I think that that can help make a success for more youngsters. I am in favour of in-school support'.* She added, however, that there was a *'point at which I might part company. If I've read the policies right, and I don't know whether I have, it would be at the prospect that all exclusions are wrong because I don't think all exclusions are wrong'.* Ms BG was also concerned at the prospect of 'sin bins' in school, although she added:

'I don't think setting up a "sin bin" in a school is the way to interpret in-school support. That's not how most of our colleagues in this City would interpret it. In fact, I think they're counterproductive. In-school support is best done in terms of money for the school. If the leadership and management are right, and the plans are right, that money will be deployed well and effectively, although it obviously needs monitoring'.

Referring to the new financial penalties imposed on schools excluding pupils, Ms BG stated this reminded her:

> 'a bit of social security fraud. It probably will drive down the number of exclusions, but there will be a cost to that as well. I'm not keen on the dowry idea. I think there are better ways and I don't think it shows a government or local authority working in partnership with heads as it should'.

In respect of the likely impact of mentoring, Ms BG argued this:

> 'depends on what the mentoring system is like. In a school that can prepare it well and set it up well, and exercise judicious guidance over the shape that mentoring takes, then yes. I think it will be very supportive for targeted pupils. Grafted on, it may not'.

Mr KM believed New Labour policy on inclusion was helping:

> 'I certainly think it's helping, erm. I know for a fact that the system set up here has helped immensely from what we had before ... We've set up a sort of "time-out" workroom as an alternative to exclusion ... Pupils will be working independently on their individual tasks ... We'd have the learning-support mentor working alongside ... After their period out there they then have a session with the learning-support centre manager who will then, erm, mentor them to come back into mainstream'.

Mr IB thought that New Labour policies on exclusion were:

> 'better than nothing. Mentoring I like, I can see mentoring working. Erm, "sin bins", you know - I don't necessarily see that that's very effective. I think there are so many dangers associated with kids just trying to get out of lessons. Er, anything that smacks of rewarding poor behaviour is a big no-no in my book. So, when a child gets the idea ... I mean, one of the kids in this school - Year 11 - goes on certain courses that we pay for like painting and decorating, and things like that. So, if a student is really causing havoc and then they can get on a special course, and they don't have to go to school anymore, they just do this instead now. I've got lots of problems with that because you've got good kids who'd love to do that. Do you know what I mean? They're not very bright, they're stuck in the bottom sets, and they're not going to get any decent grades probably - mostly Us. What they could do with is a bloody painting and decorating course. If they are not causing havoc then they can't get it'.

Ms MD thought that New Labour's policy initiatives could work long term:

> 'I think they do long term, but I don't think they do in the short term. I mean, having a mentor. I mean, how long do you have to mentor someone

before you change their behaviour, you know? I mean, sometimes it's never going to change, is it? Erm, I think it's a brilliant idea to mentor, and we've got some excellent mentoring organisations that people here come from, and I think that they are making a difference. But we're talking long term'.

Ms MD was guardedly optimistic about the introduction of in-school support units:

'Referral units? I mean, the one in our local cluster, that seems to be working very well there and, I mean, I know the government are keen. I mean, there is going to be money isn't there in April (2001) for schools to set them up. But, is the physical space alright? I mean, we're in the middle of a rebuild now so we haven't even got physical space for anything like that. Then, you've got to find the right people to staff it. You've also got to establish their purpose ... because we're not talking about the fine art of restraining somebody ... You're not just looking at something that is going to change behaviour and is going to be effective, as that is going to take a lot of setting up. You've got to have the right people to do it'.

User participation in school

All the schools had school councils to facilitate pupil participation. At Ms BG's school *'the school council would, on an annual basis, look at some of the policies in the school'.* This role did not, however, cover policy on managing discipline. Discussing her experience of her school's council, Ms PM stated that *'pupils always want things that are totally impractical for them to have, although they do use it to discuss bullying and strategies for it'.* Ms CC's school had a sixth-form council and a school council with two representatives from each form. Mr KM's school also had a school council:

'Within the school council there is one rep from each form and the form obviously represents a part of each year. And they'll meet once every half term ... Things we'll be looking at at these meetings will be things like the canteen and their involvement in that. We'll invite their opinion of the code on conduct because it's all coming down from the top and we also want it to come up from the bottom so that we are all sort of sharing the same vision of the same sort of issue. So they are involved'.

Mr IB was less sanguine about his school's school council:

'We do have a school council. There is a Year council to represent each form in the Year. It elects two representatives from among them to go on to the school council and they can reach the board of governors or heads or so forth. Personally I think it's bollocks, completely a paper exercise to make the school look good'.

There appeared to be little or no training in pupil participation in any of the schools involved in this research.

Parent involvement in management appeared largely limited to membership of governing bodies, PTAs and/or parent evenings, although some schools were introducing initiatives such as parents' workshops (to deliver study skills so that parents could help their child with their homework).

Perceptions on education, schools and teachers

Mr PH's philosophy of education is *'producing adults who are integrated, confident, skilled and happy'.* He did not feel that existing policies always helped him meet his philosophy, arguing that education:

'needs to recognise human values more in relation to standards ... flair, initiative, self-belief, sense of worth ... Things that will keep people going for the rest of their lives. A lot of what we teach ought to lead to this but it doesn't because of pressure of time'.

Having said this, Mr PH believed that his own school's priorities owed much to its head teacher:

'We have a charismatic head who has a strong sense of "inclusion" ... While we obviously seek to meet superficial statistical targets we also concentrate on seeing each child as worthwhile and on producing the best for them'.

Mr RR's philosophy of education is:

'producing members of society that are well balanced and have those skills and qualities that are going to help them to make a success of their lives and therefore benefit the country, benefit local communities'.

He did not believe the existing policy framework allowed him to achieve his philosophy, particularly because of league tables:

'I was talking to some of my colleagues, six months ago, and we were saying that the fun has gone out of it. We don't have fun - all we care about is exam results. So teachers feel the strain, under pressure to perform. It has got to the point where you have to ask "are we, the educators, doing the right thing for our pupils?". Nobody talks to the kids about it. I mean, we've got kids in Year 10 who are under stress because of the pressure that they feel'.

Mr RR stated that his own school's priorities were to improve exam results. *'But at what cost?'.*

Ms PM's philosophy of education was for each *'individual pupil to achieve their best and leave school as reasonable human beings, ready to take their place in society'*. She felt that the present policy framework does allow schools to achieve her philosophy for *'the vast majority of pupils'*. Ms PM also thought that her own school's priorities came close to her own philosophy of education and sought to develop *'decent human beings, decent citizens with appropriate examination results to go on and have a good job, life and what everybody else wants really'*.

Ms CC's philosophy of education is that:

> *'everyone should fulfil his or her potential ... and that they leave school with the best qualifications they can get and that they take away with them the best certificates that they deserve ... [And] they become well-rounded people who are going to be useful to society in whatever way they can be'*.

Ms CC thought that the present policy framework was moving in the right direction in respect of meeting this philosophy:

> *'I think it's going towards that way in that the Excellence in Cities money ... has made such a difference because we're able to use people in the way that their skills allow us to use - i.e. we have managed to pick up some very good retired teachers as learning mentors and we can tap into a pool of teachers, you know, who've got skills ... And the fact that LMS [Local Management of Schools], although we feel that our budget is not as good as it should be, at least gives you a bit of flexibility to use people accordingly ... So I think you have a bit more flexibility, yes'*.

Ms CC saw her own school's priorities as close to her own philosophy:

> *'To help everyone develop their potential ... to get up as far the league table as we can by giving the girls as much help and support to gain academic success ... and that no one leaves with no qualification - that everyone leaves with something and they're the best they can get really'*.

Ms BG's philosophy of education is *'success brings success'*. The education system should:

> *'provide as many instances of success as possible in a variety of terms as is useful. And clearly, if I understand that attainment is the ticket for the children in the next level of whatever they're going to do, I also think that on the way to that attainment, if they can reach success in a variety of things it, erm, breeds self respect, it breeds motivation and it encourages the pupils to work towards the goals that are possible. Again, the goals have to be realistic so, if the school says, "if you all work hard you will all achieve a first" this wouldn't be good. But a school that says "right, you come into school with this set of qualifications and, looking at what we*

know about you and looking at the pattern of pupils before, if things go right for you we hope that you may be able to get to this and this". I think that's a better approach than the approach that says, "yes, you can do whatever you want"'.

Ms BG thought that, on the whole, the present policy framework allowed schools to achieve her philosophy, but with the following reservation:

'There is an over-emphasis on testing. Erm, I'm happy with most of the testing. I just think it has gone a little too far in some cases. I'm not dead against it, but the role of league tables and the Key Stage 2 inflated results are the two things I'd perceive as negative'.

Ms BG described her own school's priorities as seeking to ensure that:

'each child has got his or her package of success and that most of that should be shown through their record of achievement profile, which is their badge of all the things they've achieved through school. So attainment is number one priority'.

Mr KM described his philosophy of education as: *'to enable each individual pupil to reach their potential, to enjoy their learning and realise that learning goes beyond the school gate and beyond ... I think education is lifelong'.* Mr KM did not, however, believe that the present policy framework allowed schools to achieve his philosophy:

'No, there's far too much emphasis on the academic side of it. I know the emphasis is changing, but the poor child who might be gifted in other areas ... - the child who is gifted in doing building work, or gifted with their hands, or gifted where by you can't measure it in academic terms - they are always going to find it hard and I think that's maybe where the government is losing sight of it. And the fact that it's all built on league tables and all that kind of stuff. It's singling out a lot of the pupils who fall into the exclusion category because you'll find that the pupils who are excluded - that is fixed term, permanently or in-house - are pupils who would not be in the top 65 per cent of the league tables you know. And that is because the emphasis is on the "academic". If there was some other way of measuring the abilities of some of these pupils, or just even talking to the pupils about their achievements and that, and I know it's not possible, but I think that would make a difference. So, they are losing out on all fronts these young people'.

Mr IB's philosophy of education is for:

'every student to get the best exam results they can, and I will mercilessly exploit the education system to do it ... Now, along the way, I'd like to talk about all sorts of things ... Other moral issues ... I want that pastoral side

of things to be there. But fundamentally, I know the kids are judged on results and therefore that is what drives me with all the rest of us'.

Mr IB did not feel that the education framework allowed teachers to fully deal with moral issues:

'for two reasons. Firstly, ... schools are judged far more on results, which means - although theoretically you should be concentrating on the others - you have to look at A to Cs in GCSEs and, to a certain extent, SATs ... But the moral thing is really, really hard because - yes, there's this personal, social, moral education - but I doubt the ability of most teachers to deliver it the right way'.

He thought that his own school's priorities were *'results'* and *'league tables, obviously'.*

Ms MD described her philosophy of education as:

'I don't want the school to be a little box where children go from 5 to 16, you know. It's got to be sort of related to the rest of your life. I mean, you know your kids are learning for life. It's just meeting a world of all kinds of things that you didn't know about'.

She did not think that the present policy framework allowed schools to achieve her philosophy:

'I think it's very restrictive. I think schools are bound by their exam results. They are going to be judged by those, and a lot of good schooling that went on in the past - you know, the time to chat to students ... to be involved in their real lives - has gone because everybody is trying to get through the syllabus because you've got to get good grades in GCSEs and things. And I think the government are trying to get too many things, you know. They want the citizens of tomorrow and they want them all to be brilliantly educated. They want to have great citizens. But the two don't marry, do they? You can be a good citizen without 5 GCSEs grades A-C, OK? And, I think we haven't valued ... the non-academic, you know. The carpenter or the lady who has got to clean the place, yeah? Society can't exist on Oxford Dons; it wouldn't last very long, would it? Two or three minutes and the world would be in chaos'.

Ms MD thought her school's main priority was *'trying to ... prepare the kids to fit into society - the school's society and society outside ... And we want to be known as a school that has high expectations of behaviour and academic achievement'.*

Mr H defined a 'good' teacher as someone who is: *'personable ... liked as a human being ... enthusiastic about what he or she is doing ... patient as well as well disciplined ... educated ... able to identify and analyse difficulties ... a motivator'.* A 'bad' teacher is *'where power is the main motivator ... and someone who is intolerant and lacks imagination'.* Mr RR defined a 'good' teacher as:

> *'someone who can relate well to the kids ... someone who is honest with them, who's funny and fair. The kids pick up on your mood and, as long as they know the boundaries, know how far they can go, they are not a problem'.*

He defined a 'bad' teacher as:

> *'someone who can't build a relationship with their pupils. And I've worked with some very bad teachers who I despise sometimes, and wonder why they are doing it. I mean some are hopeless ... they can't relate to people. Like a doctor without bedside manners'.*

Mr RR did know teachers who picked-on pupils and admitted that he had done it himself some years previously. Ms PM defined a 'good teacher' as someone with *'personality, strong discipline and able to get over their subject matter in an interesting way that the pupils understand. I think mainly it's personality'.* She defined a 'bad' teacher as someone who is *'very black and white and has poor discipline and, erm, really doesn't care what happens to the kids'.* Ms PM had witnessed a teacher pick on a child but considered this very rare. Ms CC defined a 'good' teacher as someone with a *'sense of humour; someone who is consistent; someone who has a good rapport with pupils; someone who has high standards'.* She defined a 'bad' teacher as someone who is:

> *'nitpicking ... one, you know, always over-reacting to trivial things; you know, people who bear malice as well you know, remembering things negatively from one lesson to the next you know; who won't forgive as well you know; who started the lesson with a grievance, really sort of "oh, last week you sat in the wrong place", "you didn't do your homework", that sort of thing; and who is boring; and poor listening skills'.*

Ms CC had not witnessed a teacher pick on a pupil: *'no, not really, no. I haven't to be fair, no. I haven't - not for a long, long time. No, no'.*

Ms BG defined a 'good' teacher as someone *'knowledgeable, aware of a variety of teaching and learning techniques, passionate for pupils to succeed, organised and just'.* She defined a 'bad' teacher as *'unempathetic, boring and unfair'.* In response to the question of teachers picking on pupils, Ms BG answered: *'I haven't seen anyone hitting a child. I've seen people do what I'd say is "pick on a child", yes. I think teachers pick on children when things aren't going well for the teacher'.* Mr KM defined a 'good' teacher as someone who:

> *'cares. A good teacher wants his children to do well, but will support them all the way along the line. A good teacher will be challenging the pupils in a learning sort of way, would always be seeking to push them a bit further, push them a bit further, erm, irrespective of their abilities. A good teacher would be an enthusiastic teacher. You could tell by the way a good teacher would have a sense of joy about the subject that they are able to pass on to the students who they are teaching. A good teacher is someone that pupils feel at ease with, and who they can speak to about how they feel about their learning. A good teacher is a teacher who the pupils would be able to put their hand up to and say, "I'm not sure how to do this" or "sir, can you help me". That's a good teacher'.*

Mr KM defined a 'bad' teacher as *'just the opposite really. Who really doesn't care. A bad teacher, basically, doesn't seem to focus ... just basically hasn't got the teaching skill to enable the pupil to progress'.* Mr KM stated that he had not witnessed a teacher seriously pick on a pupil. *'Erm, not seriously I haven't. I'm not saying it doesn't go on but I've never been in that situation. The use of sarcasm, I've seen, but not verbally abusive behaviour. No, I've never witnessed it'.* In respect of physical abuse Mr KM added: *'Er, no. I've never seen a teacher do it. I wouldn't be naive enough to say it doesn't happen, you know ... But in my teaching experience I haven't seen it. But it's not to say it doesn't happen'.*

Mr IB saw a 'good' teacher in terms of social relationships:

> *'To me, teaching is about relationships so good teachers will know the kids and get on well with them and ... there will be some sort of mutual respect. "How you go about doing that?" I have been asked. Erm, a lot of people talk about "ah yes, they've got to be good at their subjects". Rubbish! They don't have to be good at their subjects. I am a supply teacher ... I teach every subject in this school as a supply ... I am a good teacher in every single one of my lessons ... because of the relationship. But what do I do to get a good relationship with the students? Well, the first lesson I ever have with the class is always the same. I make them laugh and I make them scared in the same lesson. Scared to start with, then they get the cracking up. I crack jokes as we discuss the rules. I go through fundamentally what my rules are. I say "why do you think that is one of my rules?" And the class have to tell me why that is one of my rules. And then I say, "is that a fair rule?" So, for example, I want the children to put their hands up and wait until they are asked. Now, you can do that in one way or you can do it the way I do it which is: I'm going to pretend to be a student. I pick one student to ask the class "what's two plus two?" and, as soon as they say it, I start screaming "FOUR! FOUR! FOUR!" And I then ask the class what I did wrong and they say, "you must put your hand up". I do it in a role-play.*

I do the role of the child. I wave my hand vigorously and scream, and they say "no, no, no! You can't do that. You've got to wait. You can't just shout out". So we work out the rules together, and they laugh'.

Mr IB described a 'bad' teacher as:

'essentially the opposite ... There are certain things that really characterise a bad teacher that I hate. Picking on one child to get the others on your side - that is horrid, and I've seen it happen ... staff, er, making fun of somebody. And that child withers and the rest of the class go "ha, ha, ha". And the teacher thinks "I've got this class on my side", and they don't realise that they've just destroyed one of them. So teachers who use techniques like that, teachers who only intimidate. I hate it'.

Mr IB knew of a teacher who had picked-on a pupil:

'Yes ... When I was very new at this school, erm, the PE teacher came into the class. He was explaining that they had to fetch their swimming costumes and there was a really fat child and he said "but you, of course, will have to fetch something bigger". And the class burst into laughter. And I felt like giving the teacher a smack'.

Ms MD described a 'good' teacher as *'someone who works well with their colleagues ... someone who has a passion for teaching'*. She described a 'bad' teacher as *'someone who doesn't care about kids'*. When asked if she'd experienced a teacher pick on a pupil Ms MD replied: *'I think sometimes you snap back at kids. I mean, I snap at my own kids at home sometimes'*.

Key issues raised

Teachers' experiences of exclusions varied from school to school. In some cases there had been very few exclusions, largely in popular schools where selectivity remained and heads could choose pupils who would 'fit in'. Additionally, in the opinion of Ms BG, there was a tendency to have few 'behavioural problems' in schools with a majority of Pakistani girls. Where school exclusions were more frequent, some teachers expressed the view that many of these could have been avoided given better resources. In one particular case it was felt that the relatively high exclusion rate had been caused by the arrival of a new head seeking to prove herself as a disciplinarian by adopting a policy of 'zero tolerance' on certain types of behaviour. Many respondents believed that exclusion had resulted after other interventions had failed.

Teacher respondents presented a range of explanations for 'challenging' behaviour. Many felt family issues cause it, including taught ways of behaving, family breakdown, abuse at home or other domestic problems (financial, addiction or criminal). As with pupils and parents, teachers also felt that behaviour could be affected by either learning difficulties or pupils finding teaching sessions below their ability. Also, as with pupils and parents, many teacher respondents thought 'challenging' behaviour might be exacerbated by ineffective and/or insensitive (disrespectful) teaching. Some teachers also believed that pupils could be affected by social and environmental factors - peer-group pressure, experimentation with drugs, violence and crime, police harassment and socio-economic deprivation - which reflect some of the concerns raised by pupils themselves. A major explanation for 'challenging' behaviour raised, however, is the education system itself and the constraints it imposes on the teacher-pupil relationship and, consequently, behaviour in the classroom. The imposition of the National Curriculum and standard assessment tests, GCSE results, threshold performance pay, class sizes, OFSTED inspections and league tables were seen as placing huge pressures on the teaching profession and, in some cases, a severe teacher shortage. Such pressures, it is believed, are seriously undermining the ability of teachers to meet individual pupil needs, penalising in particular those pupils who are unwilling or unable to 'fit in' with the system. Because of this, many teachers did not feel that schools could effectively respond to 'challenging' behaviour. In particular, some teachers thought they lacked the time to discuss matters of concern with pupils, citing the need for smaller class sizes, more teachers, better teacher training, broader staff-based expertise, one-to-one counselling and effective support structures, some of which reflect the perceptions of pupils themselves. All schools had clear procedures on responding to discipline issues. These generally involved incremental stages from the teacher seeking to tackle the matter her or himself through to referring the issue to teaching teams, heads of year, the deputy head, the headmaster, the governing body or, if available, a specialist BSC. Many schools were now aiming to avoid exclusion through developing in-house BSC provision, in keeping with New Labour policy.

Respondents described different degrees of pupil/parent 'involvement' in the exclusion process, from some involvement to little or none. Where teachers claimed there was involvement this usually took the form of pupils signing behaviour contracts or pupils and their parents/carers being informed that unless there is a change in behaviour the decision to exclude will be made. In respect of support following exclusion, respondents were either unclear about what was available or described *ad hoc* arrangements for schoolwork to be prescribed, educational social workers to visit (usually reliant on the parent/carer organising) or attendance at a BSC (sometimes after the pupil has spent weeks outside the education system).

Many teacher respondents described the impact of exclusion on the child in devastating terms. There was a strong belief that exclusion could leave a child with feelings of desperation and failure, alienation and anger, and injustice and resentment - feelings articulated by the pupils themselves. Some teachers felt that it could lead children into a life of crime and drugs. Other teachers felt that exclusion could benefit a child, particularly if they are given a second chance in an alternative and appropriate setting (such as a BSC). Teachers offered varying perceptions on the impact of exclusion on the parent/carer that were similar to feelings expressed by parents/carers themselves. Some parents/carers may see it as confirmation that their child is 'bad'. Some may feel a shared sense of resentment with their child against society. Some would feel completely helpless and not know what to do whilst others may be more skilled in negotiating with the education system to get their child back into school. One teacher felt that the impact might not cause too much hardship - for instance, if it represented an opportunity to have more help in the home. Most teachers did not see excluding a child as an effective way of tackling 'challenging' behaviour. Neither, however, did most teachers see this to be the intention of exclusion. Rather, exclusion was viewed as a means of protecting the interests of students collectively (their health and safety or their opportunity to learn without distraction) by creating a breathing space within which to plan a longer-term strategy for dealing with a disruptive situation.

Teachers expressed mixed feelings about New Labour's policies on tackling exclusions. In the case of in-school support and mentoring systems, teachers felt that if these were organised effectively, with the right people in position, then they could contribute towards inclusion in the long term. Concern was expressed by some teachers that exclusions might be prevented with the introduction of the £8000 'fine'. They felt that in some cases - where the exclusion might lead to an offer of more appropriate support - this could be counter-productive. At the same time, one teacher expressed concern that BSCs offering specialist support both in-house and/or off site were being closed, removing a valuable source of support for some pupils. Overall, however, there was a strong feeling amongst respondents that broader changes to the education system - such as less stringent standard assessment expectations and greater investment in resources - were needed.

Pupil participation in school management was generally through school councils. Teachers described the kinds of issues raised at these councils: strategies on bullying; schools' codes of conduct; the state of the toilets; canteen provision. For one teacher the school council structure paid little more than lip service to pupil participation and simply aimed to give the impression of involvement. All but one school appeared to offer no pupil participation training. Parental involvement in school management appeared largely restricted to parent members of governing bodies and PTA meetings.

The majority of teachers described a philosophy of education that was about producing confident and skilled young adults, ready to take their place in society and contribute to the common good. Many respondents did not believe that the existing education framework allowed them to achieve this philosophy for all pupils: insufficient time is given to human values (such as self-belief and self-worth); too much attention is given to testing, exam performance and league tables; and too much emphasis is placed on academic success to the cost of more practical skills. This was reflected in many of the respondents' descriptions of their own school's priorities: improving exam results; helping school leavers to get a good job; academic success; seeing the school rise up the league tables; fitting children into society. For some teachers, these objectives had taken the fun out of education and were preventing them from responding to children as individuals.

Teacher respondents' definitions of a 'good' teacher included similar attributes to those offered by pupils and parents/carers: humorous; enthusiastic; respectful; a motivator; good classroom management skills; empathetic and caring; good listening skills; fair; consistent; knowledgeable about their subject and how to teach it; collegiate. Similarly, they described a 'bad' teacher as: lacking interest; intolerant; lacking imagination; non-empathetic; doesn't care; disrespectful; bears malice. A number of respondents had experienced teachers picking-on pupils.

Chapter six

The perceptions of support workers

Working with 'challenging' behaviour

Mr TH works in a BSC. His centre seeks to: *'help pupils with behavioural difficulties and some with learning difficulties'*. More specifically, the centre aims to *'prepare Years 10s to move back into school or on to FE College and Year 11s for the world or work, training or college'*. Pupils are mainly referred by the City's Exclusion Team, educational social workers or schools themselves. The average stay is 14 weeks, although this depends on various factors such as behaviour and finding a school place. During their time at the Centre Year 11 pupils attend from 9.00 to 11.45, Year 10 from 12.30 to 3.00. This time can be *'too short for some youngsters ... too long for others'*. It can also be a *'major issue with parents ... They do worry about what they do and where they are when they are not at the centre'*. Most of the activities that go on at the centre are based on the National Curriculum although *'with Year 11 we have attempted to broaden the curriculum. There are also some outdoor activities on an ad hoc basis'*. Historically, the approach of the centre has been working *'in small groups with tutor support, listening to them, good teaching, partnership with home links and encouraging good behaviour'*. More recently activities have included *'anger management and looking at youngsters' behaviour in an individual way'*. A key philosophy of the centre is a belief in *'empowerment'*. The provision should *'give responsibility to or empower the youngster in the decision-making process to help them overcome barriers to learning and give them a sense of achievement and a sense of self worth, making them feel better about themselves.'*

Mr MB works at a BSC. The centre aims to offer:

'incentives to improve behaviour. We use a mark system where each student gets a record of their behaviour and work in each lesson. They have an individual target and there's a box to say if they've met that target. And these marks are looked at at the end of each day and the behaviour discussed with the student - whether it's good, bad or whatever... And what happens then is that myself as a tutor, together with one of the teachers concerned, will talk to the student individually for as long as it takes about that behaviour ... And that's really one of the key bits with this: they can rant and rave, go up the wall, throw a chair - it doesn't matter. If they stay there, we talk about the problem. And then everything's okay. Off they go. Tomorrow's another day. So that's one of our main things ... the staying

behind to talk about the problem. It's really good. Every new day is a new day. A blank sheet. It's really good'.

Incentives offered include:

> *'vouchers - we have a tuck shop, so we have a mark system which is based on stars. Even though we are Year 10 and 11, they love to get a star. When they get 5 stars (for any reasonable piece of work, or good for them from their point of view) they will get a tuck shop voucher'.*

The centre also works closely with parents/carers. *'We contact parents/carers - very important. We spend a lot of time on the phone at the end of the day - "So and so is doing well", you know. "Keep it up"'.* All the pupils at the centre are Key Stage 4 and the focus of their work is GCSEs. Key Stage 3 pupils attend a sister centre where the focus is on reintegration into school. The centre also has students attending 6-week pastoral-support programmes, a new initiative where schools can decide they or a pupil (or both) need a break from each other through a placement. Towards the end of the placement there will be a review involving the school, the parents/carers and the pupil to decide what happens next. Usually the outcome of the review is the pupil either going back to the school or on to college. Occasionally they stay at the centre. The placement includes sessions in English, Maths and Science:

> *'but the main thrust of our work with the students is around issues of why they are here in the first place, what's gone wrong at school, what's going wrong at home, how can we make that better when we go back, or how can we improve the child's life - a lot of pastoral work, if you like'.*

Most of the centre's students attend for just half-a-day in the mornings. Year 11s do an additional one afternoon and can do up to three afternoons if they choose. GCSE choices are constrained at the centre to subjects like Maths, English, Science and Arts, and they would not expect pupils to do more than 5 or 6 subjects. Many of the pupils who come to the centre have been out of mainstream education for some time: *'sometimes we've picked up pupils who haven't been to school for months - 3 or 4 months - because they have fallen through the system'.*

Mr AB worked at a BSC. His centre served:

> *'pupils who have been permanently excluded from school ... We work with them and relocate them back into school, and all those pupils are at Key Stage 3 - so Years 7, 8 and 9. Erm, if we haven't found them a school place by the end of Year 9 they then transfer over to a Key Stage 4 centre in the city. They then carry on at that centre until either they're put back into school or alternative provision is found for them'.*

Mr DR worked as a Learning Support Manager in a school, a project funded by Excellence in Cities. He described his role as:

'*purely supportive, er, in as much as I'm outside the mainstream system which governs the working conditions of other teachers. Er, the whole idea is that I would not be perceived by the kids as another teacher. I would be someone offering levels of support within the school, within the context of education*'.

Mr DR described the levels of support that he offered pupils:

'*In the first instance it's one-to-one counselling work which is a development of the in-school support work that we did in the behaviour support service, er, and that is still the principal thrust of the job. That involves an awful lot of parental contact, and it will involve home visits and gaining as much information about the kid - the kid's street life and family set up - as I possibly can ...The other level is, because I'm a teacher, because I have been in behaviour support before for 21 years, you notice things about kids and you develop strategies which may help those kids get over some of the problems. So I look at groups of kids via classroom observations, er, information gathering from staff er and, erm, find certain common traits in those kids. Er, and I think that maybe a course could be developed that might help them. And so I offer a range of courses - intensive courses - to small groups of kids, er, on a rolling programme. There's Emotional Literacy, which effectively is what it says - making kids literate about emotions, how to handle them, er, and what good manners are; what "no" means, you know - a lot of the things that the kids should have had during normal early socialisation but missed out on. There's an Anger Management course that I run with all year groups, and I do a lot of anger management on a one-to-one as well with kids. We've just developed a Year 9 Bridging the Gap course for kids who are not seen as having management problems but could be. And I do a Year 10 Regaining the Plot course - couldn't think of a better name for it but basically those kids are disaffected, like losing the plot, and we just get them to reappraise their situation and regain the plot. And those are the courses developed to date*'.

Mr DR also offered staff development activities:

'*I run a sort of behaviour clinic for staff, a sort of drop in, er, you know: "what can I do about so and so? How can I handle this classroom situation?" But that's very much ad hoc. We haven't formalised that yet. I mean, the only time I'm involved in the school discipline system/sanction system is when the pupil is going to "timeout" - which is basically isolation. Erm, it's a sanction schools use as an alternative to a fixed-term exclusion*'.

Isolation sessions last two hours:

'They come down into this room and I do what we call a "reintegration package" with them ... The idea being that you're offering some supportive measures to help them back into the classroom the following Monday ...A kid will sit behind the desk facing the front, work will be supplied, a senior member of staff will sit at the front and observe and give the kids no room to manoeuvre. They work solid. If they don't work solid, erm, they're observed and that is recorded and, unless they are 100 per cent compliant, then timeout might be extended, they might be sent home and, saying "sorry, this is not working", we will use the fixed-term exclusion which we would have done had we not decided to give them this option'.

Mr DR stated that the Excellence in Cities project had not replaced the role of the BSS centres:

'It's actually stated by the DfEE that the idea of excellence funding at this stage is not to replace the pupil reform units, and so the thrust of it should be it's going to reduce the number of exclusions by offering a more supportive function, offering pastoral support programmes'.

Ms AF worked at a BSC. Her centre provided short-term guidance placements for fixed-term exclusions and longer-term support to permanently excluded pupils:

'Although we do have excluded pupils the main purpose is meant to be the guidance, you know. Coming in and trying to turn things around, and sending them back - usually to the same school but if not to another school ... Having said that we do have children for a long time because they sort of get stuck here for one reason or another because, you know, they can't return to school or they return and it doesn't work out and they come back again'.

Ms AF described the rules of the centre as:

'broad rules, but they're not set out like rules. I think when the centre manager interviews initially he sort of outlines the expectations and things. For example, the guidelines are all very positive. It's like "we'll be able to help you if you're willing to help yourself and ... respect others". More like a code of conduct ... But guidance students have to wear a uniform. Erm, we're not so strict with the permanently excluded ... I don't think they're quite as strict with the uniform with them so that's all made very clear, I think, when they first come'.

Ms MH was Head of a BSS centre. Pupils attended the centre from 9.30 until 2.30, longer than other support centres. The decision to have a longer day was a response to parents'/carers' concerns about the time spent by their children at the centre previously (just two hours). Ms MH believed that parents and pupils were very positive about the centre:

'We can sell it very positively. We can go to parents and pupils and we can say to them "your school has selected your child, selected you, to come on this particular course". And they want you to come on this course because the school is prepared to pay a lot of money for it, because it costs about a £1000 to educate a child here. And as soon as the child hears that they think, "gosh, the school thinks I'm worth that much!" So, it's always done very "inclusively". Also, we are a classroom down the road from 10 catholic schools ... We actually are a department of each school, that's our legal status, and it means those children are never excluded. This does not count as exclusion. It's not a punishment. They are not in trouble, they are here because they need help to put their behaviour right'.

The centre's approach to changing behaviour was closely applied to the teaching of subjects:

'Whatever subjects we teach them they are actually learning how to behave on that subject ... So, "this is how you behave in a formal English lesson; this is how you behave in a formal Art lesson". And if we practise getting that right, then they can go back and manage it in their own schools'.

87 per cent of pupils attending the centre reintegrated effectively back into school.

Mr AS worked in an in-school support centre established under Excellence in Cities. The role of the support centre was to work with pupils with challenging behaviour who were *'at critical risk of losing a place within the mainstream because of their behaviour'*. However:

'many also have learning difficulties ... and have missed out on their learning development because of time spent on dealing with their behaviour or because they have been excluded. Many are pupils who had learning difficulties, these weren't addressed properly, so they get more frustrated and their behaviour more "challenging". The school has a high rate of exclusion, reflecting poverty and the background of the pupil population, which led to the support unit being set up in the school. Its role is to maintain more young people in mainstream school ... It considers plans for enabling pupils withdrawn from classes to return. We also operate in a diagnostic way – if our efforts, inputs, don't have a successful effect ... we look at more details on why we might need alternative provision'.

Mr AS described the rules of the centre as *'agreed expectations'*. Pupils are referred via procedures described as a:

'referral wheel. At the hub is a filter group which comprises the Director of Guidance, SENCO, myself and lead learning mentors. This group meets to consider referrals. All referrals are already seen by one of heads of

department, heads of year, the senior management team (the head or deputy heads) or an exclusion has taken place in the school or the pupil has attended a "time-out centre" more than a number of times - usually three times'.

Pupils stay in the centre for a maximum of four weeks. Many will have been withdrawn from just one or two subject areas. Only a few will be full-time in the centre, many of these having been excluded from another school. Mr AS thought that the role of his centre had provoked controversy in the school:

> *'Some teachers see it as a sanction ... to teach pupils a lesson. I don't. I see it as an educational environment that looks at their needs, something that is positive and supportive, that provides a safe place in which to look at behaviour challenges. But one senior manager here stated "If a pupil has done something they should know, after being in your centre, that something has been done to them because of their serious behaviour and they should stay there until they're good!" But we are dealing with a much bigger issue ... It's not part of the sanction system ... It's a positive-action response to assist pupils. Some staff want it to be somewhere to get pupils out to. The individual needs of young people are a minor point for some teachers. I see education as a whole process ... Not just teaching a subject in a routine way. I'm hoping that teachers can begin to look at their own management style'.*

Mr AS saw his role as mainly to *'enhance what the school is already doing - not to provide an alternative to it ... An extra resource to find the answer to behaviour management'.* He was previously an external support worker going into different schools. His new position within a school had brought with it some unexpected difficulties:

> *'Ironically, I'm also in a weaker position as a middle manager in a school where there are strong feelings within the senior management team because I can be overruled in a professional way ... "I am a senior manager. While what you are saying is interesting we're not going down that route". Whereas before, when I was an external agent going into schools, I could stick to the argument'.*

The children attending the centre *'are at extreme risk of exclusion due to environmental reasons - some of those reasons are about the nature of the classroom/school experience, not just about other things out there in society'.*

Ms DB is head of an in-school support unit established under Excellence in Cities. The centre:

> *'caters for pupils with emotional and behavioural difficulties, and some of them have got learning difficulties as well. But predominantly they are*

pupils who are at risk of being permanently excluded, or pupils who the staff are really concerned about because of emotional reasons'.

Ms DB stated that the aim of her centre is *'to reduce the number of permanent exclusions from the school and to maintain children in classrooms'.* The centre had a fairly rigid referral procedure:

'The Head of Year has to have worked with the child for at least six weeks before they refer them to me. So, when the normal policies or procedures of the school haven't worked, then they would refer them to me. So, if they would normally have got an outside agency in, then that's a criteria for referral'.

Once pupils are referred:

'they don't actually have to stay in the unit ... It might be that they are taken out of lessons that are problematic ... If they're internally excluded for some reason, they might spend, say, two days in the unit. But they don't come to the unit for a prescribed length of time'.

Ms DB explained the activities in the unit:

'If they're placed in there for a particular period of time - so, if they were out of English for example - they would do their national curriculum work. They would carry on with their English work. If they're in there for a period of time, erm, they do half on the work they are set, and half they do with me. So they might do Anger Management work, if that's a problem. They would look at, erm, strategies for coping in mainstream lessons. They do a lot of work about why their behaviour is happening - what their perception of the difficulty is; what they need to go back in. So it's about half and half. And the activities are really - they're very individually designed because not all pupils have got the same difficulties'.

Ms DB explained her priorities in terms of what she wanted to achieve as:

'inclusion into mainstream lessons. I'm trying to raise awareness amongst pupils and teachers about behaviour issues, and that behaviour is the responsibility of all staff and not just a designated couple of people'.

Perceptions on the causes of 'challenging' behaviour

Mr TH thought the causes of 'challenging' behaviour were a combination of:

'parents being lax in their own discipline and who don't set ground rules; the school curriculum ... it is too academically based and not vocational enough; some teachers who don't want them to succeed; family structures ... very few of our pupils are from what you'd call "traditional nuclear families" with their natural father; and teaching approaches ... "I am the

teacher, you will follow". Teachers need to engage pupils on a different level in the class and school. They need to talk through why certain rules need to be there'.

Mr MB also thought that 'challenging' behaviour was related to a combination of factors:

'The vast majority of our students are from, erm, I wouldn't say dysfunctional families, but they are from families that have, very few have, both mum and dad (at least biological mum and dad). They have step-dad or mum on their own. Or something's happened ... We have students who have got problems, erm, related to abuse'.

Mr MB also thought part of the problem lay in the education system and class numbers:

'A lot of our students are fine when they get the attention that they require and they can get that within a class of 7. They can't cope unless they are getting regular attention from the teacher. A lot of our students require the very tight boundaries that we can provide them with and they will test these boundaries out. It's harder to do that in a class of 30'.

He stressed the problem with the education system for pupils:

'It is a mess. If I were to blame anybody, or look to see what's gone wrong, things like league tables haven't helped ... Schools are aware that these will be published. They are aware that people will be looking at the percentage of As to Cs. If they've got students who are poor attenders or who disrupt the class they're not going to be sympathetic to that student. They are going to want that student out'.

The experience of the teacher was also considered relevant:

'All our teachers here are very experienced. We've all been through mainstream, and we're all - I won't say expert but - we all know what we're doing when we're teaching these particular children. If you've got a teacher that's not quite sure what they are doing, that can lead to difficulties'.

He also thought that the curriculum was a causal issue:

'It can be seen as inappropriate ... [Pupils] don't want to do it, or are unable to do it or feel frightened about it. They will kick at it instead, behave badly, because they can't actually, or they think they can't actually, do the task that's been asked of them. And "this is the way to get out of it"'.

Another factor for Mr MB was peer pressure: *'You know - got to be seen to be the bad boy or the joker'.*

Mr AB felt that part of the cause was learning difficulties:

'and those learning difficulties aren't necessarily catered for in mainstream schools and so, basically, they fall further and further behind until, in the end ... you know they are not going to pass GCSEs. You know they've given themselves such a negative role or image so they can't do right for doing wrong'.

With others, Mr AB felt that 'challenging' behaviour was caused by a bereavement in the family: *'Over the years we've found a significant number of pupils where there has been a bereavement in the family and that's thrown the pupil'.* Mr AB also cited abuse: *'I think there are other things too. I think there's, to a certain extent, abuse at home - sexual or physical - that can be the situation. It may well be the home environment in the fact that there's not a positive male role model'.* He also saw the school system itself as a contributory factor: *'Schools cause it. I think that schools can't necessarily offer what every kid wants or needs ... I just think that the resources aren't there to do it'.*

Mr DR thought the causes of 'challenging' behaviour were:

'very complicated. You'd have to do a fair bit of social analysis to get anywhere near a reasonable answer ...There are so many factors ... Obvious ones are bad parenting in terms of education not holding a high priority for them; poor socio-economic living conditions, you know, which means survival is a higher priority than going to school and being a good boy and girl; the impact of poor teaching on the kid'.

Ms AF thought that the cause of difficult behaviour was:

'very unstable homes ...You know, when I have visited homes I've been so amazed at the level of dysfunction ... I've often wondered how children have got themselves to the centre where I was working in any kind of fit state at all. It's amazing that they actually do anything ... I feel very sorry ... I don't think the system does all that it could for them at all'.

She also felt teachers could be part of the problem:

'Yes, sometimes I think the way that, er, some staff talk to children is not what I would want to hear. I wouldn't want my child spoken to in that way. But at the same time I think you have to balance that with the fact that staff are so stressed ... I don't think they have the energy or the personal resources to teach children who are having difficulties in the way that they probably need to be treated - that is, therapeutically really ... I don't think teachers can always be fair either. Not because they don't want to be fair

but because they have a number of children in their classroom and they can't see everything all the time, can they? And I think, I mean, all children hate injustice, don't they? Every person hates injustice'.

Ms MH thought that a main cause of 'challenging' behaviour was peer-group pressure:

'So many of our children will be classified as the "class clown", and they're the ones that the others will all egg on, you know. Here, we don't get manipulators - we get the manipulated. And they're the ones that are daft enough to go and do it, you know. So there's a lot of pressure on them to maintain that, you know. "I'm the hard one in the classroom. I'm the hard boy here"'.

Behind this Ms MH thought that learning difficulties might also be a factor:

'I think that there is a lot of pressure on young people who have perhaps got learning difficulties. And I think that they're desperately frightened of being shown up as being stupid or thick. And it's much better to have a reputation or be naughty than being stupid or thick ...We tend to have a habit as well in this country where we set children up. If a child isn't a very bright child and has behaviour difficulties we look at them as a special-needs' case because we don't want them spoiling the chances of the others to get their GCSE As. So then you're a "special needs", or the one up from that, you know - the bottom set really because the special needs are quite well looked after. But you get the bottom set and in that group you then get all these naughty children, and children who aren't very bright, and so what kind of subliminal message is given then? "If you're not very bright you must be naughty. If you're naughty you're not very bright" ... We're giving all the wrong messages, I think'.

Ms MH also thought that, in certain circumstances, *'there are teachers who cause children to behave badly. Teachers who use sarcasm, who use put-downs as a means of control ... There are grave difficulties there for young people; grave difficulties'.*

Mr AS was unwavering about the causes of 'challenging' behaviour:

'It's about exposing weaknesses in the education system, the roots of exclusion, issues in the classroom and classroom management. What we learn here has to be shown on a wider scale because there may be more things you have to act on. If we're telling the truth about wanting to include the most challenging pupils we need to look at what we do about organising secondary schools in the future. The children who challenge because their behaviour doesn't fit the pattern - many are doing it because there are things wrong with the pattern. They are more able to reject, or not toe the

line, or take the standard route and accept "this is the way you've got to be". Yes, some are disruptive. But some are the most intellectually challenging of the system and we should listen to what they're saying. We have quite a few pupils who came to us and can define exactly why they feel they are being excluded. While amongst it there is the admission that "yes, I did talk to the teacher like that, in that tone of voice. But he talked to me like that tone of voice. I refuse to accept it". There's a tremendous pride in it - some adults see it as wilful adolescent cheek, but some of these pupils are reduced to tears when they believe that their desire to be shown respect is not being taken seriously within the system. And the biggest issue - because there is a narrower curriculum requirement than there used to be (I began teaching in the 1970s when you could introduce all kinds of alternatives and do things school-by-school and there was the possibility to respond on a broader level) - now many teachers can't respond on such a broad level with the breadth they'd like to to meet the needs of the pupils. So, for example, if a child has an attention span of say seven minutes - so every lesson plan for this child needs to run in seven minute cycles with time inbetween - that has a planning implication for a teacher. And while all the learning theory suggests that you should never throw in hour-long slogs, a lot of lessons are pitched at around those kinds of levels. There are huge deserts of learning experience that some children are going across. And if you take the combination of learning difficulties along with their concentration span and everything they've experienced about why they should/shouldn't work, and you ask them then to go through that ... without negotiating with them ... and then you're surprised when a minority is disruptive! I find that hard to understand when we ourselves would be disruptive in those situations'.

Mr AS went on to suggest that:

'It's clear that the impact of the National Curriculum is partly blocking successful inclusion ... If you give more flexibility to the schools to meet the specific needs then I believe there are a load of talented people in schools who would snap out of that very narrow approach and you would see some very exciting things happen. But it's very difficult if you're trying to measure standards ... That has been used by a lot of people as an excuse to narrow down what they do ... There's a lot of comfort in that. "I know exactly what I'm trying to do. Our school is trying to achieve a 10 per cent increase in its A-Cs in GCSEs. That's our raison d'être. Oh, we've also got to include these challenging children. Oh, that means it'll be harder to achieve the target because it's disruptive ... If you, Mr AS, could just take them for a little bit longer". I also know, in legislation, there's plenty of opportunity for schools to try alternatives. It does actually say, "look at Key Stage 4. Go for difference if you need to, go for disapplication. Don't feel that you're tied by the National Curriculum". But it's so unfair to actually

say that to staff when the main way you're measuring their progress is by one aspect. So most staff are unwilling to get involved in that kind of flexibility. Seems to me that an obvious lesson is for politicians to look at this ... Teachers would love to do more for children ... That's why they came into teaching – to do the broader thing, the education of the child. And they can see that with a different approach - with a level of patience and understanding for the challenging child - he or she could achieve ... "But actually, when it comes down to it, he or she is actually disrupting my lesson. And as I'm now being put under all kinds of pressure from my head to do this, that and the other with my subject results, I've decided that's where my focus of attention is"'.

Ms DB thought that one cause of 'challenging' behaviour for some pupils was the fact that they were studying at an inappropriate level:

' The pupils that I'm working with at present that are attached to the centre - a lot of them are probably functioning at a level above what they're academically getting and they get bored and frustrated and they start to act out. So they're in the wrong class or ability level. They might have been put down because of their behaviour, so they get bored and their behaviour has deteriorated'.

She thought that another cause of 'challenging' behaviour was the pressure teachers were under:

'I think that there have been, erm, a lot of new initiatives in the last few years. I think teachers are under enormous pressure to deliver the national curriculum, performance management, and all these targets. And that comes from the top down. And that pressure is transferred from the senior management to the teachers, and the teachers transfer that pressure to the pupils. The pupils haven't got anywhere to put that pressure, so they, erm ... I think they are not coping, erm, with the demands that schools are making of them. And in that, I think, a lot of the fun has gone. It seems to be all slog and a lack of individual attention that maybe they [pupils] should be getting'.

She also thought that family background and home circumstances had a role to play:

'I think some children live in family and home circumstances that are completely incompatible with the demands of school life ... A lot of our children [98 per cent from Asian households] have to go from school and then spend two hours at the Mosque. So they are perhaps working to 7 o'clock at night and then they have to do their homework. And education is quite highly valued by our school population and many of the families. There's no outlet for children to be children. And for the girls, when they

get home they have a lot if work to do. They have a lot of cooking. They have a lot of helping in the house. A lot of sewing. And I think they're very tired. There's also a dietary factor. A lot of the children don't eat properly. They're up at 5 or 6 in the morning [to help with domestic chores]. They don't have breakfast. They have quite often rubbish for lunch. Or they don't have lunch or very little, erm, and it's a long day. So, it's a kind of combination of a lot of factors'.

Perceptions on tackling 'challenging' behaviour

Mr TH thought that *'for some youngsters the shock of exclusion has worked ... They've been told they were going to be excluded so many times and given so many second chances ... It can be a tenderising experience'.* He felt, however, that there were better ways of supporting pupils with 'challenging' behaviour such as *'pastoral-support programmes, with no agenda to get the pupil out. Help could also come from other pupils in the school, perhaps through the school council'.* Overall, however, Mr TH did not feel that schools had the necessary resources to tackle the root causes of the problem: *'There isn't enough time ... More time is needed for teachers to take a breather during the working day ... to relax, recharge their batteries'.* Moreover, *'other resources - like extra help – only have a limited effect. The working environment of teachers is such that any problems become more extreme'.* Neither did Mr TH feel that teacher training provided the necessary tools to manage 'challenging' behaviour. But then again, *'There isn't an answer ... Many of the good ideas come with practice. There should be people who can share their ideas'.*

Mr MB thought that there should be more emphasis on training teachers in behaviour management:

'We do in-school support and there are things like frameworks for intervention where teachers are going in and working with teachers in in-school support. There are a lot of "improving behaviour packages" that you can buy now that schools seem to be opting for that are, you know, generally good things. They give a structure to classroom management which is needed in any school and which maybe, in the past, some schools were lacking'.

He did not think that schools always had the resources to tackle the root causes of difficult behaviour:

'Some of them are impossible for us to tackle. If Dad's an alcoholic, what can we do really? It's really a case of trying to get the student to be able to cope with the situation. To develop strategies, to develop coping mechanisms if you like, to deal with a lot of those things, including peer pressure or the inappropriate behaviour of a teacher or the curriculum or whatever'.

Mr AB distinguished approaches to tackling learning difficulties from approaches to tackling behaviour problems:

'Is it because of the learning difficulties? If that kid can actually go into the classroom with their peers and be able to do the work, will they still exhibit the behavioural difficulty that they have done in the past? And if the answer to that is "no they won't" then you've cracked it by cracking the learning difficulties. But there are other pupils who either have or haven't got learning difficulties, but they have got behavioural difficulties. And in the same way as you need someone to say "you're able to do the work now because we've made the work slightly different for you - not necessarily easier, but different in terms of special needs", you then need someone to come in or someone to actually be with them to say "right, now I'm with you to overcome the behavioural difficulties" ... I could imagine the situation where someone would go in and sit with a pupil - they don't need to sit with them because they've got learning difficulties, they can actually do the work, but they may be easily distracted or whatever - and someone with them to say "no, don't get distracted, get on with it". But I can interpret that as a massive resource, erm, you know'.

Mr DR did not think schools had the necessary resources to deal with the causes of 'challenging' behaviour:

'It's not just a physical resource it's a human resource as well. And I think, when you look at most established schools, you've got a level of staff who belong to a different era and haven't quite made the adjustment to what's actually happening now'.

He thought that education policy's preoccupation with academic standards prevented schools from attending sufficiently to:

'the social development of the child ... I don't think sufficient is done in schools to address some of the social imbalances that you get in society ... You've got to point the finger at the government for having set up such massive bureaucratic systems ... which teachers are far too preoccupied with'.

Ms AF thought schools should try and give pupils more support, in particular by helping them to overcome a 'bad reputation'. She felt some pupils were being blamed for things they had not done:

'That happens all the time because they're children with reputations ... And that's another thing I always try and work on. I say to them "it's unfair, but you've got this reputation. And you've got to undo that. And in order to do that you've actually got to be better than good. You've got to be better than

*the rest of them in the class - to stand out as being better - to reverse that".
And it's hard ... Sometimes they feel that they've done really well and of
course then they just put a toe out and the whole thing comes apart ...And
that is very hard. And I tried explaining that to staff as well and to say "you
know, when a child is coming back in after a guidance place, erm, you
know, please can we have a fresh start?" But again they don't get it'.*

Ms AF did not feel schools had the resources to manage 'challenging' behaviour.
She also thought teacher training did not prepare staff adequately.

Ms MH thought that schools should use incentives to address 'challenging'
behaviour:

*'We have a code of conduct and the code of conduct is a very simple one
and it says, "our target is to show respect for others". And we say the code
of conduct applies to everybody, the adults as well as the children ... There
are also normal classroom rules which are: we are prepared to begin work
promptly; we listen to the teacher; we raise our hand to speak; we avoid
distractions; we work hard. And so long as they follow those then we have
a very simple points system and we say to them "5 points - they are yours,
we give them to you at the start of the lesson and you can keep them or you
can throw them away. But the only way you will throw them away is by
breaking the code". And the points actually become very precious to them
because they know it represents they're okay ... The pupils then get
certificates every week ... and those go into their records of achievement so
they are considered to have value ... They do like having the points. They
get very upset if they lose points because they're theirs. What we're saying
all the time is "you are making the choice here, it's your choice; your
behaviour is yours. I don't make you behave in a particular way. My job
here as a teacher is to facilitate the circumstance whereby you, as the pupil,
want to work. But I am not in control of your behaviour. You are". And
therefore we have to teach them self-discipline really. That's the biggest
lesson anybody wants because, you know, there are teachers in schools who
are very hard and strict and so on, and they can control classes and kids do
exactly as they are told in that room. But that's not actually training their
students properly about behaviour management. They need to learn it for
themselves'.*

When asked if schools had the necessary resources to tackle the causes of
difficult behaviour Ms MH replied:

*'The necessary resources are people really, aren't they? It's the right
people we need desperately. Plus the size of the classrooms ... I tell you one
of the things I feel strongly about and that is that schools, erm, certainly in
inner-city areas, are now getting Excellence in Cities money. Er, a lot of
schools are now setting up units of their own. It's what they do with those*

that I'm concerned about. I think that there would be ways of using those units more wisely than just using them as sort of "throw-out" units, where if a child misbehaves they just get chucked out of class and into them. I think rather than just say let's throw them out because they're misbehaving in that particular class ... I think what I'd do is use the unit in a very different way ... I would offer a course for ... I'd take eight of the bullies in the school and I'd do an assertiveness course for them on a Tuesday morning. I'd take eight of the victims of bullies and do the same on a Wednesday morning. I'd take eight of those very quiet little girls who nobody notices - they've got no self worth at all, and when they're teenagers and are desperately seeking love, and they confuse sex with love, and so they end up as a teenage pregnancy ... On a Thursday I'd do an anger management workshop and on a Friday I'd do a bereavement counselling session because again, I think a lot of our children are showing reactive behaviour to loss ...'.

When asked if teacher training provided the necessary tools to tackle 'challenging' behaviour Ms MH replied *'No, not at all'*.

Mr AS outlined an empowering approach to tackling 'challenging' behaviour:

'Part of our preparation with pupils is to prepare them with some understanding of the pressures that the system is under ... But even that is controversial because some teachers believe we shouldn't be sharing any of that kind of thinking with pupils. The idea of trying to get them to think about what others in the classroom are struggling with, as part of the reason why they should control their reaction. It's OK if it's to do with the behaviour of other children. But it's certainly seen by some teachers as unprofessional if we are also asking them to consider "what's happening with the teachers?"; if they imagine "what's happening in the teacher's mind?; what do you think the teacher is trying to address?". "Well, the teacher's trying to teach a subject and it's two weeks to the exams ... And they're under pressure". But some teachers resent the fact that a kid might turn round and say "I understand why you're actually under a bit of pressure because we've got our exams in two weeks' time". It is actually interpreted as cheek in some cases ... Actually, a criticism that was levelled at us was that some of our explanations about children's behaviour that we might give which are perfectly reasonable - "this child is reacting to these tensions, here are the tensions and here's the evidence. We've been in and seen it". And we put it all very clearly. It's actually very difficult for some teachers who are feeling very threatened, very deskilled - perhaps for other reasons - to argue back at all. And therefore there is fear of our contribution because it illustrates their weaknesses when all that they were expecting was a child better prepared to do the work that the school was setting them'.

Mr AS thought schools needed to give more attention to the learning process as a whole rather than merely focus on the difficulties posed by the pupil:

'If you're talking "inclusion" it is not just about making a child fit what's already there. Inclusion only works if there is an equal change in the processes into which you're putting this child. Because you have given that child tools to deal with their behaviour, and those tools are not just solely about saying "I promise to be good. I'll sign this agreement". I mean, to hear some people talk, a signed agreement to behave well is the major tool when that means absolutely nothing. And so, it is crucial, if people are going to understand what we're about, if they are going to look at the question of exclusions properly instead of in this safer way which doesn't get to the root of the problem - "zero tolerance". The same behaviour processes that you're using in working professionally to support a pupil with their difficulties - the sensitivity that we're presumably expected to use - need to be adopted in exactly the same way with anybody in that working setting'.

In other words, the role of monitoring behaviour should also extend to staff:

'The majority of pupils who work with us are in some ... of their mainstream lessons. And those teachers have to also monitor the targets that we are setting here. So, we're getting results from them that we can look at. So, a pupil who we've worked on to keep in their seat, to learn to sit for longer ... we then set those same targets for staff in the mainstream to be looking for. That pupil is given marks between 1 and 5 - 1 is "not achieving", 5 is "achieving" - and you can work out a rough, objective set of results which the people who manage these big pictures love to see. They like to see those and they like to see things graphed, and they like to see things "evidenced" (they call it). And it is evidence. And so it means that the child who has that difficulty will have also succeeded in most of the teaching settings of the mainstream. And the difficulty comes when we're down to the subject area where actually it was happening the most ... If I knew the answer to that then we probably wouldn't need these kind of centres because, I'm afraid, I can't answer easily what you do about the intransigent teacher who holds up their right to manage in a particular way and - despite all the information given, despite all the advice, despite the work done with the pupil, actually insists, in a professional way, on maintaining a routine that is going to retain that challenge. Or at another level, the one who refuses to admit that they have a totally chaotic lesson situation'.

Ms DB suggested a similar approach to managing 'challenging' behaviour:

'Well, I do quite a lot of work about, erm, educating them about what anger is. What the triggers are and what they do as a result - the acting out behaviour, why that causes a problem in the lesson and what they can do instead. So it's really about, erm, getting them to control what they do after they are angry. And perhaps get them to do something that's not going to cause a major disruption in the lesson, or get them sent out. So they might, erm, write something down on a piece of paper - they have little notebooks. So they might write the incident down. They just learn ways of talking to the teacher differently ... I think it helps them stay in mainstream classes. I think it gives them strategies to deal with individual teachers - because I haven't actually yet come across one pupil who has problems with all the teachers. So, sometimes it's just a matter of, erm, getting them to understand not just their behaviour but other people's behaviour as well'.

In terms of tackling the wider social factors affecting pupils' behaviour Ms DB did not feel schools had the necessary resources:

'No. But I think that schools don't necessarily see it as their job to tackle issues that are around home. Erm. With quite a lot of the children I work with - when I talk about home circumstances to the teaching staff they're completely unaware of the background of these children. I mean, some of them actually say they don't see it as any of their business. It's not their job to take that into account. I don't think either that, erm - I mean, the school I'm at, there's no parents' room, there's no, erm, I think that the pastoral system doesn't have the time, erm, available to, perhaps, erm, talk to parents, erm. They might get 10 minutes or contact is made over the phone ... erm. I think a lot of schools say parents are welcome in at any time, but the reality, erm, is not that. Erm, there's no comfortable places for them to sit or just, erm, space and those kind of physical resources really, and human resources like time'.

Ms DB did not think teacher training was providing the tools to manage challenging behaviour:

'No, I don't think it does at all ... I do a talk for postgraduate students once-a-year, erm, at a local university and that's usually about an hour-and-a-half. And this year, because I asked for more time, I had 3 hours, and the students told me that, in the whole of their 4 years' training, that is the only input that they have on working with difficult behaviour. I think they do work on child development, but I don't think they actually have very much input on dealing with classroom behaviour management. And I've talked to a lot of students at the school I'm at now and they've said they were never given any input at all'.

In respect of INSET for existing teachers Ms DB argued:

'There's a problem here. I offer some training on behaviour management but a lot of staff have said to me that they won't come on it or put their names up for it because that's like admitting that they have problems with behaviour. And they don't want to be perceived as that: as having a problem; as not being able to cope'.

Perceptions on the impact of permanent exclusion on the child

Mr TH thought the impact of exclusion depended on how quickly pupils were reintegrated:

'If they don't get back it's devastating ... if they're not given a second opportunity. The worse scenario is where a youngster comes out and feels aggrieved they shouldn't have and feels they deserve another chance - and they aren't given another chance ... They are the most difficult to manage in the centre. There is an embarrassment about finishing off your education at a BSC for many families ... So the long-term consequences are very damaging'.

Mr MB felt that the effects would depend on the individual pupil:

'I would say for the majority, and I'm probably biased, but I would say that the vast majority of students that we take - that come here - it benefits them ... The majority would do better here because they wouldn't survive in the mainstream. The ones I do feel sorry for are the students that we have - and we do have half-a-dozen at the moment - who have been excluded for things like possession of marijuana. And you look at it, and you read what's happened, and they've taken one spliff into school. And I would say that the school has panicked and the child has been excluded. And when we get them they are perfectly able, perfectly capable, perfectly respectful ... And those are the children where we look and think "well, why aren't you in mainstream, why are you here?"'.

Mr AB thought exclusion often leads to crime: *'Without a doubt I think there's a danger of a descendent spiral into crime'.*

Mr DR again felt that the impact of exclusion would vary, although he generally thought there could be wider benefits:

'It will depend a lot on the level of disaffection in the kid. But it's not only about the kid, it's about the kids that have been left behind and sometimes, to say to the class of Year 9 kids "so-and-so's behaviour was totally unacceptable and we're not going to stand for it, and they have been excluded" can have a positive impact in terms of behaviour management on the rest of the pupils. And that aspect cannot be ignored'.

Ms AF thought the impact on the pupil would be damaging *'because it is a huge rejection'*. Similarly, Ms MH:

'I think the long-term impact is terrifying really for a lot of pupils. There are pupils who manage it - they cope somehow and they pull themselves round and they go to another school ... But I think for the long-term effects of permanent exclusion, if you look at any of our prisons they are full of people who were excluded at school. And they will say, "I failed at school."
... I think once you've been told you're a failure as a child, how do you drag yourself up from that? I'm very well aware that there are certain children who cannot do mainstream education - it's not possible. I mean that's absolutely right - and there should be specialist provision. But we've got to get away from this, erm, "kick them out" because, I think, it has a terrible, negative effect on every child who's ever been thrown out of school'.

Mr AS again expressed grave concerns about the impact of exclusion:

'It is a disaster in that child's life and people who imagine that it's just a new opportunity really get up my nose because it's an appalling experience. And every permanently excluded pupil that I've ever talked with ... talks about how they actually felt about being rejected. And although they may talk with a different edge - some will talk in a challenging way, some will talk in a despairing way - the actual impact on that child is like saying "you don't fit, you'll never fit, you are an outsider" ... It takes them a long time to gain a trust in somebody ... I think the cost is huge to them in personal self-esteem, and then of course all the other knock-on effects which are well documented. They reject much more easily other requirements of a society that's let them down'.

Ms DB perceived similar effects:

'I think they possibly would feel very resentful towards the school system. And I think maybe long-term that would be passed on to their own children. I think they possibly feel quite let down because there's a lot of emphasis placed on exam results, and then you don't get a job. So I think it reinforces a lot of negative thoughts about themselves'.

Perceptions on the impact of permanent exclusion on the parent/carer

Mr TH suggested that the impact of exclusion on the parent/carer would vary. For *'some it's an embarrassment, a traumatic experience. For others it justifies their own opinion of their child's behaviour'*. Mr MB thought the impact would depend on how quickly the pupil received positive support:

'Once they [the parent/carer] hear positive things about their children, and they can see that we're not on anybody's side except the student's - we want what's best for the student - they see what we're doing is fair and they will back us to the hilt really'.

Mr AB thought the impact on parents would vary from:

'low self-esteem on their behalf by failing as a parent to frustration with the authorities, school, education department, whoever it might be, that, er, you haven't done anything for him ... you're not really interested in them, you don't really want them to be in mainstream and stuff'.

Mr DR thought the impact depended on the extent to which parents/carers valued education:

'There's those households where there is no precedence whatsoever, you know, so that the kid could be successful without having to complete education ... But a subjective answer would say that most parents feel ashamed that they're responsible and often it's the first time parent and child get to talk together, you know, because everything has built up so much'.

Ms AF saw different impacts. For some:

'I would say it doesn't impact very greatly, except they are, perhaps, stuck with the children at home. On that level they find it very irritating. But then I think a lot of parents find it very difficult to do the necessary, you know. They tend to come from a very dysfunctional family so again, it's generalising, but you know - it's usually the mother or the carer or sometimes it's the auntie or the grandma – erm, I think they find it difficult to know what to do'.

Ms MH saw very negative impacts:

'I think that parents ... feel very cheated by society if you like, and certainly by education. I mean, I get quite a lot of phone calls from parents from all over the country saying "you know, my child has been permanently excluded - I don't know what to do", erm, and I think what's sad is that they're going through a panic ... and they can feel very anti-authority and they feel that they themselves are being criticised because of their child's behaviour and often they don't know what to do. There may be some official who comes along and says, "there's a sheet of paper for you to fill in, this is what you do", but they need somebody to talk them through it. They need the human touch to say "right, this is what's going to happen next, these are your rights, this is what you can do, here's a telephone number", you know, "those people will help you". And that can be very helpful'.

Mr AS described some terrible effects:

'There are some who rally around their child and become actually more excluded themselves from society because it's then "us against the world". So there's those who are determined to defend their child in quite spectacular ways sometimes ... Then there are those who reject the child. There are some who cannot take what they see as a personal failure and a personal shame. And so, for instance, I've certainly been party to emergency requests to social services to respond to an incredible, angry rejection by a parent following a permanent exclusion. It's a very damaging thing to happen for all parents. I tell you this as well; it's usually handled appallingly badly. It's not often, and I've been in meetings where a permanent exclusion has been upheld for instance - I've sat as a governor - and I think that the system is a desperately unfair system for the parents in that situation, erm. I think we wouldn't put up with it in a legal sense, in some respects, because they are so heavily outnumbered. The whole personal experience is that we are all in the dock together and this bunch of worthies, who call themselves governors, who probably never showed any interest in their child at all - such is the nature of the work now - are busy saying "we've listened to the evidence and your son isn't going to stay with us" ... I just think how astonishing we are at the ease which we allow that to happen in society. I think it's tough on parents and the disaster, if you like, is the kind of ripple effect'.

Ms DB thought that exclusion caused parents/carers tremendous stress:

'I think a lot of excluded pupils get into a lot of crime. And certainly, in the area that I work, there are a lot of children who get into all sorts of dodgy stuff on the streets. I think that's very difficult for parents: to know where their children are or who's controlling them. They very quickly and very easily get involved with a lot of things that are going on on the streets, and the parents don't have any control of that ... especially if they've got young children to look after or they're working'.

Perceptions on the effectiveness of exclusion

Mr MB was ambivalent about whether exclusion was an effective way of changing behaviour:

'I can't really say "yes" or "no". It may, you know, make children see the light. But just the exclusion? No, I would say. Just the mere fact that they're excluded, I would doubt it is going to change their behaviour. The things that happen after they are excluded may well. In terms of coming here or another establishment may well change their behaviour'.

Mr AB thought that excluding a pupil could help to change behaviour for some. However:

'Of those that it would be effective with you maybe needn't of gone that far. For example, a pupil is involved in violence with a member of staff or whatever and, to a certain extent, that's a permanent exclusion. That kid comes to us and we're asking, "what happened in school?" "Well I hit a teacher" or whatever. "Do you want mainstream school?" "Yes I do". And basically it's then a question of finding a mainstream school the kid can go in and where he can operate successfully. And, you know, that's just been a one off. I think with some kids there's almost a "nothing's going to happen anyway" mentality. You say all these things are going to happen, but then you say "permanent exclusion" and "where do we go from here? Do you want to go back to school?" "Yes I do". "Right, okay". And you can put them back and, if that had been the mentality of the kid then that is relatively easily solved. Because of that I think for the majority of pupils who get excluded from school - that in itself doesn't solve the problem ... I think it does for some'.

Mr AB argued that guidance placements, three-weeks out of school on a managing-behaviour programme, were probably more effective than exclusion:

'I think the guidance placements we have here, which are presented in a positive way - at least most of the time - have been a very effective deterrent that has been used, although we don't present it as a deterrent ... I've got a girl I'm working with at the moment and the school is very concerned that she's gone back into school ... She was talking in golden terms about the centre ... she was saying it's really good ... the teachers have got time for you and all the rest of it. Even then, you say, "so would you rather have that, or go back to school?" They want to go back to school. They want to go back to be with their peers, and I can understand that. It's like a cooling off period before going back into school. And I think that could be done on a wider level'.

Mr DR felt that exclusion may be an effective way of confronting 'challenging' behaviour: *'It can be [that] the stigma of exclusion was sufficient for that kid and parent to confront the issues that caused exclusion and to do something about it'.* Ms AF did not believe that exclusion was an effective way of managing difficult behaviour:

'I just think it's an effective way of getting them out of the school's hair, isn't it really? I think that's more about the school saying "we've really, as far as we're concerned, tried everything that is in our means or at our disposal". And there probably aren't enough means at their disposal'.

Ms MH felt that excluding pupils was a *'totally ineffective'* way of changing behaviour. Instead she felt it was more important to teach pupils how to behave.

Neither did Ms DB feel that exclusion was an effective way of changing behaviour. Instead:

'I think that part of the problem is the problems are perceived as just to be with those individual children. And I think it's a wider issue ... A lot of teachers don't see that they have a part in contributing to the problems in lessons or the disruptive behaviour. They always see that it's the pupil that has the problem. I worry about [support] units that adopt that philosophy. You know, that these children in front of them are all "problem" children or they're all disruptive. So they're not working with the teachers to look at what part they play in it as well'.

Experiences of reintegrating excluded pupils

Mr TH said that the rate of successful reintegration from his centre (around 25 per cent) was very poor. The majority of pupils were re-excluded:

'There are many factors why youngsters get re-excluded or find themselves outside the system. One of the major ones is the terms on which they're allowed back into school ... the "trial" if you like. This prevents a youngster having a sense of belonging with that school and consequently, I feel, the school are not as committed to them as well and, for that reason, they quickly turn round and come out. So, the major factor is the terms of their return'.

Mr TH also highlighted difficulties he had experienced when seeking to return pupils to mainstream schools:

'I have absolutely major problems and I could go on for the next hour about the reasons why they can't take on the pupil. The list is endless. It is most frustrating. This past term [Winter 2000] we have successfully achieved one school place for Year 10 - so there are at least seven just kicking their heels. It's an on-going problem in the City ...There are school reasons like the school is in special measures or due an OFSTED visit. But so many other excuses have been given'.

While legally a school must accept a pupil if it has an available place, Mr TH claimed that there was:

'not enough LEA vigour to make sure the legal position is upheld. I feel desperate for some programme like Panorama ... to set themselves up and contact schools with the idea that they were pursuing school places and see what response they get'.

He did think having assertive parents/carers helped pupils return:

'It shouldn't be about whether the parent is assertive, or knows how to pursue their legal rights, but it is. The issue of why some youngsters go to a

support centre and others go straight to another school is because, in most cases, the parents insist they don't go to a centre'.

There is the added problem here of parents of excluded pupils going to schools with places:

'which is not very fair. It does perpetuate difficulties these schools are having. A few lucky schools have waiting lists and if they exclude they can quickly fill their place with someone from that waiting list'.

This was a concern raised by Mr MB. While some pupils re-enter mainstream schools with places:

'if they have places then they are probably another bad school so their problems get worse. And this is what is happening. This was always the danger of LMS - that you would get these, if you like, "sink schools"'.

Mr AB commented that schools were reluctant to take pupils from his centre although:

'some schools are more cooperative than others. Some schools will offer a place on a basis of "if you take from us then we'll take from you" ... Other schools will be very reluctant to ...take a pupil who has been permanently excluded'.

Ms AF saw the problem of integration in terms of pupils' adaptability. She felt that some pupils might never adapt to mainstream school:

'It's difficult to generalise but I suppose an inability to sit still, concentrate, focus, erm, a lack of understanding and respect for the system, you know. An inability to do what mainstream school requires, which is to do as you are told. They struggle with doing as they are told, erm, and they do see teachers as authority figures. And the feeling, and again I'm generalising, but it's a feeling I've had that they are, well, "nobody's telling me what to do" sort of'.

Ms AF described the future for such pupils as *'grim'*. She also recognised, however, that the type of school was important:

'There are certain school environments that they certainly would do better in than perhaps others. I mean, for example, I go into a community school just round the corner and although it is technically a mainstream school it really doesn't feel much like a mainstream school. Erm, it's very small, the groups are small, and the staff and pupils are on first name terms and so, as I say, it comes under the mainstream umbrella but really it's very unlike a mainstream school ... So that type of school is one which certain fragile children would sort of fit in really'.

While schools with places are technically expected to take pupils applying, Ms AF felt that some selection remained with heads considering the wider situation in their school:

'Schools really vary. Some schools are much more willing to accept pupils from the centre ... I do think it's a bit of a lottery really ... What year the child is in? What the child's reputation, background is? You know, ... some schools just won't look at certain pupils. They don't have to because they're full technically, so they know they don't have to. And then there are schools that complain that they are asked too much. They feel there's an imbalance ... I think you can understand it if a school does have falling rolls and they are having to fill up their numbers with pupils who are excluded just because they have places available. It's not going to help their falling rolls and they will have other pupils leaving because the school is filling up with problem pupils'.

Mr AS raised concerns about some of the rigid criteria used by some schools on returning pupils:

'I worry when you do have a set of criteria; it's a two-edged thing because it's possible for somebody who wants to slow the process of return to say, "well, they haven't met all those criteria". It's a bit like the signed agreement - all schools seem to have a formal, erm, signed agreement you can just get from the computer every time a kid is coming back in from an exclusion, or every time you want to tie a pupil to a set of arrangements. And they get the same letter, and that letter has the six expectations of the school and you sign it - you say, "I agree to keep all those". And then it's possible to keep a kid on a behaviour policy like that for months because you can say "you've done five of them - but you're still no good on the sixth. I'm just not prepared yet to let you out"'.

Ms DB explained problems experienced by pupils after their re-integration:

'They often find that the, er, they're under pressure from their peer group about the fact that they've been out. Or they are under pressure from their peer group because, quite often, the child that has come out is the one that has provided the entertainment for the class. So they are often under pressure from the class to, erm, do that again. And that's quite difficult for the pupil. Also, sometimes the teacher doesn't necessarily accept that the pupil has changed or has done work on their behaviour'.

Perceptions on New Labour's policies on school inclusion

Mr TH thought some recent initiatives on inclusion (such as in-school support) *'could help if run well and they look at the reasons behind difficult behaviour ...*

But if they become a "punishment zone" then no'. He believed, however, that effective approaches to school inclusion must be:

> '*more child centred, and challenge school policy and what was happening in that school. Some of these youngsters are voicing what the silent majority are not always capable of saying'.*

Mr MB believed the encouragement of in-school behaviour support units could be an excellent idea:

> '*if they can get them properly staffed and get them the right sort of ethos ... in that it is a support unit and it's not a "sin bin" within the school where naughty children are sent for a few weeks in isolation and then come back and miraculous things are meant to have happened to the student - which chances are won't have'.*

He was concerned, however, about the introduction of "fines" for schools excluding children:

> '*The fines system means that schools won't exclude and, the worrying bit will be, what will happen to these students? I personally think that there needs to be a very close monitoring of whether students are attending because, although schools will be pulled up if their attendances fall, they may decide it is worth that child not coming into school ... I go into mainstream and I know of a student who is Year 11 ... It has got so bad that they're not turning in, they are truanting a lot of the time. When they do go in it's not a happy time for them or the teacher who is trying to teach them. Eventually, they stop going, they end up with no GCSEs and the school has not wanted to exclude them, not wanted to lose the money. So this child has gone into this missing persons sort of area'.*

In response to such problems Mr MB's centre had developed a:

> '*3-week improving behaviour course that schools can opt to send their students to. They have to pay for both this and the 6-week course, but what schools in our area have done is banked together to form a group and they have all put so much money into a kitty, which guarantees them so many places for students. The disadvantage to that, maybe, is that come the end of the year when they know they have places they haven't used they might decide to send certain students on it, which they wouldn't have done in the first place. But I think, on balance, it seems to be working well'.*

Mr AB thought new in-school support centres could be a good idea '*if they are used properly ... But, unless they are careful, they will just become sin-bin camps and sin bins don't work. We've had them in the past'.* Mr DR explained how the south-west area network of schools in the City had decided to use its Excellence in Cities funding to finance pupil-support programmes at BSS centres rather than '*set up their own exclusion units/learning support centres*'. He did feel that budgetary factors were now becoming increasingly important in deciding how to manage difficult behaviour. In particular, the decision to exclude:

'*is now based on a financial consideration, er, which may well mean that you have to retain a kid because your budget is used up and you cannot afford to exclude them. Which will then beg the question "well, that kid was excluded for doing that but this kid isn't going to be because we can't afford it". So we're bringing in a moral dimension there'*.

Mr DR felt that such cost considerations:

'*makes a bit of a mockery of the situation. If at the end of the day, if whatever level of support you are offering, you have to think, "well, can we afford to do this?" But it also makes a school think that little bit more creatively perhaps, a little more widely as to what strategies they can use in order to keep a kid in school'*.

He thought that some recent policy changes would improve things and offer:

'*very dynamic and much needed methods that are long over due and which we are only just beginning to see … It's going to take time to filter through a school system, but the mentoring and learning-support centre aspects are, I think, vital, especially in a city-area like this'*.

Ms AF also thought that government policies were moving in the right direction:

'*It's such early days with mentoring though … One school I used to go into … I think in fact the site manager was the mentor for quite a few of the lads and, I think, just because of his personality and that he was always there he related well to the boys. That seemed to be working quite well'*.

Similarly, Ms MH was cautiously optimistic about the new initiatives: ' *I think they are still in the very early stages and I think there is still a lot of confusion about them but I think that they will do yes, yes'*. Mr AS saw differential responses in schools to the government's new initiatives:

'*across the City different Learning Support managers work in different ways … [sound of school-bell ringing followed by comment from Mr AS: 'you get that too, don't you? Another automatic response expected. The bells!'] … But they are coming round as the months go on of the whole Excellence-in-Cities' programme in the City to a similarity of concern'*.

Mr AS felt that the way the new initiatives were being implemented in the City depended largely on the relative academic success of the school:

'*I benefit here because it's a school where the levels of success, academically, are at a fairly low level against the national average. There is an acceptance that there are behaviour management issues or there are classroom management issues or there are learning issues, erm, there are attitudes-to-education issues that kind of legitimate some of my comments. Doesn't mean that they are believed by the teachers all the time but they know they can't dodge the fact that actually there are a lot of under-achieving children. I was discussing with another Learning Support Centre Manager of a school where there is a high academic success rate and he was pointing out to me why he couldn't follow all my ways of taking on issues about classroom management because, he said: "You've got to remember. I've set up a centre in a school where they believe they're doing everything right. Where the teachers are getting good results. And so it's actually, I believe, tougher for me to keep a difficult child in this comfortable setting than for you where at least there is a kind of expectation that there will be difficulty'.*

Ms DB thought that recent policy change was more effective *'because it's keeping pupils in the mainstream school. It [achieves] continuity ... I think it's very difficult for pupils to change schools half way through their school life and to be accepted into another mainstream school'.*

Perceptions on education, schools and teachers

Mr TH described his philosophy of education as:

'the socialisation of the young. Making them reach their potential - be it academic or vocational. Trying to get society to accept that the two are equal and deserving of the same reward when they've left school'.

He believed the present education framework placed too much emphasis on the academic. Mr TH's own priorities in terms of what he is trying to achieve are:

'inclusion. I know this City supports the principle of inclusion and that gives me great strength in my own work. I feel that many parts of the City haven't taken on that principle and that influences my priorities ... I sometimes feel I'm swimming against the tide. The philosophy and the practice need to come together. The practice needs to enable the philosophy to succeed. It's not at the moment'.

Mr MB defined his philosophy of education in terms of producing *'well-rounded citizens'.* Under the present framework he was not sure schools were allowed to achieve this:

'I'm not sure if it does, erm, in terms of time allocated to some of the things that we feel are of use, and we feel we need to give to our students. We know that our students benefit from our pastoral programmes. We know that, we see it all the time, and with that in mind we have tried to take it into mainstream schools. And we offer mainstream schools, erm, different

courses, one aimed at school refusers and poor attenders, and another one aimed at Year 9, 10 and 11 Key Stage 4 students who are displaying behaviour problems ... But we do find that schools are ... I wouldn't say reluctant, but ... they've got pressure on them from the curriculum to find time to offer these courses. But not all students - obviously not all students - need them. But there is a significant minority, I would say, who do benefit and who do, if you like, need these things".

Mr AB's philosophy of education is *'success for every pupil ... whatever their level of ability - you know, background or whatever'*. He did not think the current education system helped schools to achieve this:

'It's all about GCSEs rather than ensuring the pupils are successful at their level ... There's no scope for working with difficult kids ... There are a lot of circumstances, you see, like the pursuit of GCSEs now as a symbol of a good school, you know, that doesn't help ... At the end of the day, how is a teacher seen as successful? By the number of GCSE passes. How is the school seen as successful? By the number of GCSE passes from A to C. And there are other people, working away in the background, working with difficult kids, but basically managing the kids. And you know, that doesn't get recognised'.

Mr DR's philosophy of education is *'to deliver the widest possible education to the child. To give a child the best possible chances in life'*. While Mr DR did not think that the present system allowed schools to achieve this he thought that things were changing in the right direction with new initiatives aimed at addressing both the *'behavioural shortfalls in school'* and *'the gifted and talented - the other end of it. Yeah, I think we've got a better chance now than we had three years ago, but it needs developing further'*.

Ms MH's personal philosophy of education is:

'that all children should be forgiven ... So, effectively, there is a consequence of an action. Forgiveness demands that you make arrangements for what you've done that are right. But having done that you then turn round and say "right, now let's make a fresh start"'.

Children often find that they can't have a clean slate:

'That's what really bothers me and I think that when that begins to happen, and they feel themselves being labelled, there is nothing they can do. And because we tend, in schools you know, maybe we do it for the right reasons, but we tend to, in schools, to have things like "on report" systems. And when a teacher sees that, they psychologically think "I must be on the lookout for something negative about this child". And so they find something negative instead of ... "progress". And we have "progress"

[reports] so the child can see themselves exceeding. And again, I go into a lot of schools and ... look at their annual file on a child your assisting. And you see all these reports that have been stacked in this kid's file. And you look through them and nearly all of them have got "excellent", "very good", "excellent", "very good". So why is that child still on report? Because we want to maintain it. How many of us can be 100 per cent perfect 100 per cent of the time? We should be looking at what is reasonable'.

In response to the question of whether the present policy framework allowed schools to achieve her philosophy Ms MH replied:

'I think it means to, yes. But I don't think it does, no ... because I think there is so much pressure and competition amongst people for it to be a success in terms of very narrow-minded rules and guidelines, you know ... How do you measure success? ... I don't want to be measured on how many children I get through GCSEs. I deal with children with behaviour difficulties, and they are only at Key Stage 3. But if we could get away from that competitiveness mentality to say that every single child is a wanted child. You have league tables for schools. But are they realistic? Each child deserves education ... We concentrate on the wrong things really. If we could concentrate on the difficult children, and make them feel welcome and part of the school ... And every other child is going to benefit from that by the positive way in which you treat them'.

Ms DB defined her philosophy of education as:

'All children should be included. Education is for everybody. But I think in terms of inclusion, it's not enough to just say, "we are an inclusive school". I think if a child feels included that's when inclusion is working. If they don't feel included, erm, then it isn't an inclusive atmosphere. I think all children should be included but I don't think that's a possibility ... I think schools should be willing to adapt and change to include pupils. And I think the general thinking is that pupils should adapt and change to fit the school. So I think that there's a long way to go before all children will be included in the education system'.

Ms DB did not think that the existing policy framework allowed for inclusion:

'I do think as well that education should not just be about the national curriculum. There's a lot of education that should be going on in schools that is completely missed. There's too much emphasis placed on certain core subjects of the national curriculum and, with the publication of league tables, then that's putting a lot of pressure on schools to better their last year's results. And so, you know, a lot of emphasis and resources are going into, you know, Maths, English and Science. And gone are the vocational

courses, erm, the kids who aren't high flyers can, erm, be interested in. There's nothing for them. So, I think, certainly higher up the school, that's when you get a lot of disruptive behaviour. Because they know they're not going to achieve. The teachers don't want to bother with them because they're not going to achieve. And they get lost'.

Mr TH described a good teacher as *'flexible, encouraging, open, warm, inventive and (it seems so obvious) having a sense of humour'* and a bad teacher as opposite. He had seen teachers picking on pupils in his mainstream days and getting away with it. Mr MB defined a good teacher as someone who:

'cares for their students. And that not only includes the curriculum, but cares for the whole ... really cares what happens to their students, not just in terms of academic results but in terms of how they are as a person ... If you care for somebody you provide everything that you can for that student, including good lessons and support, and discipline and whatever you see that student needs'.

Mr MB defined a bad teacher as someone:

'not being able to see the bigger picture. Not seeing the child and seeing the behaviour. Not really taking the behaviour personally and reacting against that behaviour with, you know, er, it's very hard. I'm not going to - you know, I've been in mainstream - I'm not going to start saying mainstream are bad teachers. I mean, we get teachers who aren't as good as other teachers in our service. I know that I'm not as good as other teachers ... There are teachers who struggle, but it's the system's fault for not picking them up and giving them the support'.

Mr AB thought a good teacher was one with:

'a good sense of humour and, I think, the ability to talk to the kid in their own language. And by that I'm not talking of English or whatever. I'm talking in terms of having some idea of what these kids are about ... It's always been a thing in my mind that the vast majority of teachers that come from middle-class backgrounds and work with working-class kids don't know what's going on out there'.

Mr AB described a bad teacher as:

'someone who doesn't know their subject matter to the extent that they should. On the other hand, for the vast majority of our kids, you don't need to know geography to A-level standards to get through to them. The geography that they need you to know, most teachers would be able to do that. Just being a page or chapter ahead of them. But basically, what will engage the kids is the fact that they've [teachers] got the time to present it

to them in a way that they understand or whatever. I mean again, I don't know if it's relative but I use the example to one of the schools I went to and they said that, for example, regarding kids with learning difficulties, if you give pupils something to do - a task to do - and they don't understand it - the vast majority do but one or two don't - you don't then tell them exactly the same thing all over again. You kind of tell them slightly differently and, if that doesn't work, then you try and tell them slightly differently again. It seems to me a bad example of teaching is that they tell people to do something and then, if they don't do it, they tell them to do it again in exactly the same way rather than using a different way of telling them. Telling them in a louder voice is not the way to do it'.

Mr DR described a good teacher as: *'someone who ... goes home at night and feels happy with what they've done during the day, but that assumes so much ... Someone who can maintain the interest of kids'.* In contrast, Mr DR sees a bad teacher as:

'someone who doesn't want to be there, someone who cannot understand a rapport with kids, erm. A teacher is someone to me who can go into a room with a group of 30 kids and establish a rapport. If you can't do that you might as well not be in the bloody job to start with, and it doesn't matter what subject you're putting over - that has to be your number one priority, that you can relate to kids'.

Mr DR had witnessed a teacher pick on a pupil but added that *'the "picking on" bit is more to do with the pressures that the teachers are under - in other words, I cannot recall a situation of teacher maliciousness ... I'm not saying it doesn't exist'.*

Ms AF thought it was difficult to describe a good teacher:

'I think that is so hard and it's very difficult to find a common denominator because it's something that you know about - especially when someone isn't it! I have friends who are extroverts who are good teachers, and some who are very quiet and, you know, going back to my own experience with my own teachers, you know, the people I remember as good teachers - I can't think what they had in common except that they had the quality to engage me ... They could connect with children. Now, whether that's through their subject or personality, it's people who make a connection in some way'.

Ms AF described a bad teacher as:

'someone with very fixed ideas, not very broadminded, sort of unable to see the bigger picture perhaps ... And that's another thing I find I'm often saying to staff, sort of trying to fill them in on a few details of the pupil's life: "do you realise that so and so goes home and mum's not there, mum's

working, mum doesn't get home till 10 o'clock in the evening". And they don't know this kind of thing ... The teachers who aren't so good will sort of, well, you know - "she's got to sort herself out". It's almost like, "in life ... you can't expect someone to be behind us all the time". And they can't sort of feel for that child. There's no feeling, there's no empathy I suppose'.

Ms AF had not seen any violence against a pupil:

'But I have certainly heard what I would call abusive language ... I've been in the situation, in the school, where I've been in a room where the children come to see me and this has been going on in the corridor outside. And it's not obvious that I'm in my room ... I can't believe it. The teacher was unaware, mmmm ... I mean that, having said that, I've heard a lot of teachers talk to children in a way that I wouldn't dream of talking to them ... But then again, I have to keep remembering ... that I'm not a mainstream teacher. I'm not under those pressures'.

Still, Ms AF raised some concern about certain teachers:

'Most of my information comes from the children. Obviously, I bear in mind that children exaggerate. They tell lies. But I've still heard enough from a variety of children, and it's mostly the same [teacher] names that come up time and again. And the stories are too similar, you know, from different children that you know it's obvious that something is wrong with the way that some staff talk'.

Ms MH described good teachers as:

'people who facilitate the circumstances whereby the children want to work and want to learn, erm. They make children feel safe and secure and if all the children feel safe and secure then they can throw away the rubbish that's binding them down - this fear of "the world's out to get me"... They think about each child in their care. They don't treat them the same, they treat them as individuals ... So I may well say to this person, erm, who has difficulty staying in their seat, "I'm going to let you get out of your seat three times every lesson and no more than that three times. And I'm going to remind you when you've only got one more to go so you can use it wisely" ... Or another child who is a potential need [attention seeker], and you'll say to them "now, I'm not going to ask you the first question that you know the answer to. I won't ask you the first time, I'm going to ask you the fourth time - but I want you to keep putting up your hand because you know that I will ask you the fourth time". And they can go "great! I am actually getting that attention that I need". So instead of them putting their hand up and then saying "you never asked me, you're always asking someone else first". That can go'.

Ms MH thought bad teachers were those who: *'don't like children very much, erm ... The worst teachers for me are those who are very, very sarcastic and put children down, and don't show respect'.*

Ms MH had seen a teacher pick on a pupil:

> *'Yes, yes. Unfortunately I have ... I have seen a teacher, you know, glue sniffing with children. I've been aware of violence but haven't seen it, er. But certainly verbal violence, quite frequently, or what I would consider verbal violence. Anyway, I consider it abuse the way that some teachers speak to pupils. And I think schools handle it very badly. They protect each other ... Our children will tell you about it ... One child came to us and said that he was sitting in a dinner hall with his friends and a teacher said to his friends "don't hang around with him, he's a loser" you know. He carried that around with him. He felt very angry by it. He felt humiliated. He was ashamed in front of his friends. Another boy came here and said a teacher had said to him "you're the sixth worst boy in the school" ... I believe often it [abuse] doesn't get dealt with. I mean, one of our outreach staff has heard some very horrendous things of teachers saying things. I'm sure what we need to do is to make sarcasm and put-downs as anti-social as racism, as nobody would admit to being racist now, would they? No teacher would dare say, "well I'm racist, and I don't care". And in the same way teachers should not be allowed to get away with bringing down children'.*

Ms DB defined a good teacher as:

> *'one that has got a relationship with the pupils, that recognises that they are teaching individuals, and makes a relationship with them, rather than goes in there to just deliver information. A good teacher is somebody that has enthusiasm for the people sitting in the classroom and wants those children to be involved with the whole process'.*

Ms DB thought that:

> *'there's a lot of teachers who have poor relationship skills themselves, or who are frustrated by the whole system and maybe take that out on the children. Who have kind of lost what the job is about ... I see a lot of teaching going on which is very worksheet based, or it's very "read this chapter and answer the questions". Bad teachers, or just bad teaching?'.*

Ms DB also stated that: *'I can think of lots of instances where I've seen and witnessed children treated violently [by teachers]'.*

Key issues raised

Support for pupils with 'challenging' behaviour took one of two forms: in-school support and out-of-school support in BSCs. Support can be seen to operate from two perspectives: one, as a sanction, such as the 'timeout' unit in Mr DR's school where pupils have to learn compliance; two, as a way of raising pupils' awareness about their behaviour. In some situations awareness raising applied to both pupils and teachers, reflecting the notion that pupils' behaviour is rooted in a two-way relationship. Much of the support offered pupils is in the form of small group work (isolation in the case of sanctions) involving counselling, and anger management and emotional literacy courses.

As with pupil, parent and teacher respondents, support workers saw the causes of 'challenging' behaviour rooted in, in some cases, learning difficulties and insensitive teaching. As with teacher respondents, support workers also believed that family problems (family breakdown, abuse at home, 'bad' parenting, etc.), social and environmental issues (peer-group pressure, socio-economic deprivation, etc.) and the education system itself (class sizes, the preoccupation with academic standards, league tables, the inflexible National Curriculum, etc.) were causal factors. There was also the view that many pupils who 'challenged' were amongst the most intellectually gifted, able to articulate their dissatisfaction with the education system.

As with the teacher respondents, the support workers did not feel that schools had the necessary resources to tackle 'challenging' behaviour. In particular, they believed teachers had insufficient time and expertise. Moreover, there were broader issues - such as poverty and problems at home - where it was felt that teachers were unable or unwilling to get involved. In effect, in many cases, the support given to children is to give them coping mechanisms for dealing with these broader social problems less confrontationally. Amongst the suggestions for supporting pupils with 'challenging' behaviour included: peer-group support through school councils; pastoral-support programmes; sharing good practice; teacher training in behaviour management; distinguishing between learning and behavioural difficulties; less pre-occupation with academic standards; ceasing to stigmatise pupils with 'bad' reputations; reducing class sizes; reviewing the learning process; monitoring staff behaviour; anger management courses; greater liaison with parents; more willingness amongst teachers to do anger management training.

Similar to teachers, support workers felt that the impact of exclusion on a child would depend on how quickly they were reintegrated, either in a BSC or mainstream school. Some felt that the BSC support available often benefited the child longer-term. In respect of pupils who don't reintegrate quickly for whatever reason, the impact of exclusion was considered devastating - such as a spiral into crime and/or loss of self-esteem and trust. They also felt that the impact of exclusion on the parents/carers could vary. In some cases it could be devastating, further marginalising an entire family from the 'mainstream' by reinforcing notions of an unjust society. In other cases it was felt that the parent/carer might turn against their child, having reinforced notions of their 'badness'. Where a child received early support it was felt that the impact might not be so severe. As with teachers, most support workers did not see exclusion (on its own) as an effective way of dealing with 'challenging' behaviour. If linked to other support, like a BSC or guidance placement, exclusion may be the first step towards tackling behavioural problems, although it was perceived by some respondents more about getting an unruly child out of the school system. Respondents described a number of difficulties they have faced when seeking to reintegrate a pupil into school. Quite often, schools seek to maintain their 'market' position by refusing to take an excluded pupil. The assertiveness of the parent/carer may help overcome this refusal. Even where schools have taken pupils back, the terms of their return (such as a rigid behaviour policy) have made it difficult for the child to remain reintegrated. Another concern raised by respondents is the situation of the least successful so-called 'sink schools' with places that accept excluded pupils, which may perpetuate existing problems. As with the teacher respondents, support workers were ambivalent about New Labour's initiatives on school inclusion. Most thought that moves towards in-school support could be beneficial if run with the right ethos and the right staff. There was, however, some concern that they were being used, in some instances, as punishment zones or 'sin bins'. Respondents were also concerned that the introduction of financial penalties on schools that exclude might encourage practices amounting to 'hidden exclusion' - for instance, turning a blind eye to truancy.

Support-worker respondents described philosophies of education that were very much about encouraging all children to reach their full potential, but acknowledging that this might be either academic or vocational. It was generally felt that the vocational aspect of education had become less valued in British society. There was also a strong sense of inclusion in some of the philosophies defined, including the view that schools needed to adapt themselves more to difference and diversity within the pupil population. As with teacher respondents, most support workers did not feel that the present education system allowed their philosophy to succeed. It was felt that the emphasis on academic success, the National Curriculum and league tables left little scope for teachers to respond to the different needs children might present in the classroom. Support workers' definitions of 'good' and 'bad' teachers were similar to those described by pupils, parents/carers and teachers. 'Good' teachers were defined as: flexible; encouraging; open; warm; inventive; humorous; caring; empathetic; engaging. 'Bad' teachers were seen as basically the opposite. Some support–worker respondents had seen teachers pick on pupils - sometimes violently - and get away with it.

Chapter seven

Findings and policy implications

Findings

Comparing the perceptions of pupils, parents/carers, teachers and support-workers involved in this study, a number of clear, common themes - with implications for social policy – can be identified.

- First, it would appear that many school exclusions are for relatively minor[1] or unsubstantiated incidents and, therefore, quite possibly avoidable. Certainly, the excluded pupils and their parents/carers expressed strong feelings of social injustice about exclusions that were shared by some teachers and, more so, support workers.

- Second, while many teachers and support workers advocated a philosophy of education with inclusion at its heart, the majority of respondents did not feel that this was achievable in the present system. There was a strong sense amongst teachers and support workers that government policy was focused on a narrow 'quasi-market' notion of education - academic excellence achieved through competition between schools - that worked against the creation of an inclusive school environment.

- Third, the majority of all four respondent groups appeared to acknowledge that 'challenging' behaviour was often caused by social and environmental factors - child abuse; learning difficulties; urban deprivation; violence, crime and drugs; the problematisation of 'youth'; racism; insensitive policing; labelling and stigmatisation; family problems. Additionally, many respondents felt that these problems were exacerbated by school factors - peer-group pressure; disrespectful and non-empathetic teachers; unresponsive governors; and a lack of resources and effective support. Instead of responding to these difficulties in a strategic way, schools generally feel that they have little option but to exclude in order to protect their reputation.

- Fourth, pupils and their parents/carers in particular, but also some teachers and support workers, felt that the decision-making process of exclusion permitted them little support, advice or involvement.

---

[1] Steve McCormick, a newly qualified teacher, depicted 'poor behaviour' as 'more irritating than outwardly disruptive' (*The Independent Education*, 10 January 2002, p.11).

- Fifth, most respondents did not believe that exclusion was an effective way of dealing with 'challenging' behaviour. Many felt that this was not the purpose of exclusion anyway, and that it was more about protecting the school's 'market' position by ensuring that the majority of pupils achieve academic success to raise the school's league position.

- Sixth, the short-term and long-term consequences of exclusion for the child and parents/carers can be devastating, particularly when the child is out of mainstream or supportive provision for some time (which remarkably is often the case). Several of all four respondent groups spoke of the child's loss of self-esteem and trust, and/or feelings of fear, pain and depression. There was a strong belief amongst some teachers and support workers that exclusion could lead children into a life of drugs and/or crime. Once excluded, the child and parents/carers can spend months without support. Teacher respondents were (at worst) unaware of what support was made available after exclusion or (at best) described *ad hoc* arrangements for homework to be set or some degree of educational support service to be provided. Effectively, in most cases, the excluded pupil is simply abandoned by society. In time, they will often gain access to a BSC. While pupils were generally positive about the provision offered by a BSC - particularly because of the small class sizes and empathetic teachers - parents/carers expressed concerns about the short attendance time and the amount of work set. Still, these centres can offer pupils a 'fresh start'. At the same time, however, support workers highlighted alarming difficulties faced by themselves, pupils and parents when seeking reintegration. Quasi-markets in education and the retention of selectivity mean that excluded pupils are often refused re-entry into popular schools. As a consequence, less popular schools with places that accept excluded pupils may be adding to the problems they already face. Additionally, once accepted by a school, excluded pupils can face barriers to reintegration due to onerous resettlement practices such as rigid behaviour plans or stigmatising record files. Also, whilst the pupil respondents generally retained clear aspirations in terms of their future careers and/or family life, there was a feeling amongst some that their exclusion from school would be a major barrier to achievement. It would appear, therefore, that a potential cost of excluding children from school is lifelong exclusion.

- Seventh, both teacher and support-worker respondents expressed mixed feelings about New Labour's initiatives on tackling school exclusion. There was general agreement that new in-school support centres could be more effective if organised and staffed by people with the requisite expertise and ethos. In particular, if they acknowledged that 'challenging' conduct was a two-way process that also involved the role of the teacher in pupils' behaviour, and that this was addressed, then they could have some success. It was also felt, however, that attention needed to be given to the social and environmental factors (discussed above) shaping a child's lived experience and, subsequently, their behaviour. Additionally, there was some concern (and evidence) to suggest that a number of teachers saw new in-school support centres operating as 'punishment zones', used merely to isolate and discipline 'disruptive' children. Teacher and support-worker respondents also highlighted concerns about New Labour's introduction of 'fines' for schools that exclude. In some cases it was felt that this could lead to 'hidden exclusions', such as condoning truancy. There were also fears that fines may prevent a child with difficulties from gaining the right provision for him or her – for instance, by being placed at a BSC with expertise in emotional literacy or anger management. One teacher respondent believed such centres were threatened with closure as a result of funding being directed at in-school support. Ultimately, however, most teacher and support-worker respondents did not feel that government policy on school inclusion went far enough. Many called for more far-reaching measures, such as less stringent standard assessment expectations, the abolition of league tables and threshold performance pay, a more flexible National Curriculum, greater investment in resources to ensure smaller class sizes, and more attention to 'behaviour management' in teacher training.

- Eighth, pupil respondents' expectations of school discipline and 'good' teaching contrast little from those of their parents/carers, teachers and support workers. Most pupils understood and considered 'sensible' their school's rules and codes of conduct, as did most parents/carers. Furthermore, in defining what makes school enjoyable, most pupils stated the attitude of the teachers. In defining the characteristics of a 'good' teacher all four respondent groups described similar attributes: humorous; respectful; good classroom management skills; empathetic; caring; non-racist; good listening skills; fair; enthusiastic; captivating; motivating; consistent; knowledgeable; collegiate; flexible; encouraging; open; warm; inventive; engaging. What the pupil respondents most wanted to change about schools was the way their teachers taught and for this to reflect these attributes. Most parents/carers, teachers and support workers agreed with this view of 'good' teaching.

- Finally, none of the pupil respondents, and few of the parents/carers, believed that they had had an effective role in shaping the way their schools operated.

Policy implications

An inclusive education system cannot be realised in the context of a society driven by neo-liberal orthodox values. Competition among schools based on narrowly focused criteria for success is perpetuating divisions within and between secondary schools. What is needed is a radical rethink about the purpose of education in Britain and the way teaching and learning is delivered. Many teacher respondents spoke of a philosophy of education that saw its purpose as creating the citizens of the future. Good citizenship is not solely about people having excellent academic qualifications or vocational skills. It is also about having empathy and tolerance for others. Moreover, if we are to place inclusion at the heart of the education system, that system needs to recognise and accommodate difference and diversity. At present it does not. So what needs to be done?

- First, we need to dismantle the national curriculum and current arrangements for measuring 'success' in education. These are placing unnecessary burdens on teachers and pupils, and act as a disincentive to co-operation between schools in tackling both exclusion and the growing educational divide. In their place we need a more flexible curriculum and system of assessment, incorporating the needs and interests of a broader constituency comprising local education authorities, schools, parents/carers and pupils. This would require authentic structures for parents/carers and pupils to participate in school matters, facilitated through independent advocacy - effectively, the encouragement of genuine 'citizenship' practice in schools.

- Second, teacher training and teacher performance assessments need to place greater emphasis upon the teaching and learning *process* (qualitative factors) and not just academic *outcomes* (quantitative factors). Quality teaching and learning, as this research shows, is largely dependent upon the attributes of the teacher, and whether they are empathetic and respectful. It is about the process of teaching and learning. If we want to create a society respectful of 'citizenship' (as New Labour claim to) then children are the citizens of today and the future. School should be one place where empathy and respect for others – aspects of 'good citizenship' - are fostered. In a sense, 'good' teaching should be similar to 'good' parenting. Whatever a child's behavioural traits, a 'good' parent will listen to and negotiate with them – they would not just abandon them. The same principle should apply to 'good' teaching, and parents/carers should have the right to insist on this.

- Third, the current practice of abandoning children from the education system for months without support - which is having a devastating impact on the lives of many young people - should be outlawed. All children have the right to an education.

- Fourth, the practice of selectivity by schools, which contributes to social exclusion by perpetuating the advantages of middle-class neighbourhoods, should discontinue.

- Fifth, social policies need to address the structural underpinnings of exclusion rather than merely respond to the behaviour of the child, which in many cases may be a valid reaction to social injustice. Focusing on 'behavioural problems' constructs the child as 'victim', a feeling often internalised by the child as low self-esteem and resentment. This focus also sidesteps the need for policies to address poverty (wealth redistribution), disempowerment (opportunities to participate in decision making) and environmental deprivation (neighbourhood renewal, and the provision of facilities for children and young people).

- Sixth, government needs to abandon its neo-liberal economic orthodoxy and accept that an authentic quality and inclusive education system requires investment to ensure that teachers have the adequate resources, skills and qualifications to meet the learning and support needs of all children.

- Finally, although the sample is limited in terms of size and representation, this research offers sufficient indication that a further and more extensive study into the lived experiences of school pupils and their teachers is warranted to discover the extent to which the concerns raised are experienced more widely.

Conclusion

While our findings support much of the existing evidence - for instance, the profound sense of injustice and denial of social opportunity experienced by families, highlighted in Hayden and Dunne's (2001) report - our recommendations go much further. This is because we feel that many existing policy recommendations fail to address exclusionary processes within the education system. Hayden and Dunne, for example, suggest action to deal with the symptoms of an exclusive education system - for instance, specialist support, to include teams of social workers, to ensure children conform to dominant notions of 'appropriate social behaviour' (Hayden and Dunne 2001: 85). Such measures fail to acknowledge education's role in perpetuating unequal power relationships and social injustice, or the legitimised 'anger' felt by many children and young people. As Peter Leonard has argued, '*anger is a gift*' and that collectively '*anger emerges as a moral protest at injustice*' (Leonard 1997: 162). What we are advocating here is collective resistance to the oppressive practices within the British education system, built around a shared understanding of the utility of that system for contemporary power relationships. How such resistance might arise is the task we turn to in the final chapter.

References

Hayden, C. and Dunne, S. (2001) *Outside, looking in: Children's and families' experiences of exclusion from school*, London: The Children's Society.
Leonard, P. (1997) *Postmodern Welfare: Reconstructing an Emancipatory Project*, London: Sage.

Chapter eight

Understanding secondary school exclusion: the production of docile bodies

Background

This final chapter aims to illuminate our understanding of school exclusion through a theoretical examination of the issues raised by this research. The theoretical framework of analysis chosen largely draws on the work of Michel Foucault and his observations on the utility of education systems for maintaining dominant power relationships (Foucault 1977). The choice of this approach followed the transcription stage of the research. What is evident from the perceptions of the pupils, parents/carers, teachers and support workers involved in the research is that children who do not comply with the expectations of a highly prescriptive, instrumental and uniform education system are at risk of permanent exclusion and all the disadvantages that this brings. Even though a child's 'non-compliance' is invariably a rational response to conflict situations or personal difficulties, the education system, due to its primary concern with managerialist targets, is unable to accommodate this behaviour. Consequently, the system pathologises such ways of behaving as 'abnormal', in need of treatment or punishment. The argument here is that the main purpose of the British education system is the production of docile bodies that will comply with and sustain dominant socio-economic and political power relationships. This contention will be supported by illustrative quotes from the respondents to this research that mirror Foucault's thesis on 'projects of docility'.

Projects of docility

A major contribution of Foucault is his questioning of dominant ways of thinking that see historical development as following a linear path towards greater rationality, human enlightenment and social progress. Foucault believed modern societies' rationality was not necessarily more enlightened or progressive than our predecessors. Indeed, he believed that it had potentially developed into a more limiting and inherently 'violent' form of rationality. He shows how the regulatory practices of contemporary institutions - although different from the past - are even more oppressive and cruel because they are subtler, hidden and all encompassing. In particular, contemporary state intervention has become a major tool of social control, asserting power over the body by:

'... ordering, measuring, categorising, normalising and regulating. In disciplining the body, persons as subjects become governable, thus marginalizing the need for coercion in the regulation of populations.'
(Usher and Edwards 1994: 92).

Foucault describes how, during the eighteenth century, physicians, politicians and technocrats became increasingly interested in what he termed *'projects of docility'*, ventures in creating bodies that could be *'subjected, used, transformed and improved'* (Foucault 1977: 136). Foucault was not saying that interest in manipulating bodies was something new to the classical age - it was evident much earlier in monasteries and armies - but what did appear to change was the scale of such control and the growing recognition in its economic (productive) and political (obedience) utility. Foucault identified a number of disciplinary schemes, including the organisation of individuals in both space (through enclosure [spatial confinement], partitioning [individualised spaces], functionality [defined site-uses] and ranking [by location] and time [through timetables and schemas of behaviour that routinised ways of behaving]. These schemes aimed to accrue maximum benefit while minimising waste and disobedience, in the name of economy, efficiency and effectiveness. These schemes or *'general formulas of domination'* (Foucault 1977: 137) emerged over time from different origins. They provided an organisational theory common to prisons, factory management, army barracks, hospitals and schools, making it possible to exercise discipline over any individual subjected to these institutions. Specifically in respect of schooling, they *'were at work in secondary education at a very early date, later in primary schools'* (Foucault 1977: 138). In the eighteen century, the Christian educator Jean-Baptiste de La Salle planned classrooms to distinguish pupils by their *'progress, worth, character, application, cleanliness and parents' fortune'* (Foucault 1977: 147):

> *"'In every class there will be places assigned for all the pupils of all the lessons, so that all those attending the same lesson will always occupy the same place. Pupils attending the highest lessons will be placed in the benches closest to the wall, followed by the others according to the order of the lessons moving towards the middle of the classroom ... Each of the pupils will have his place assigned to him and none of them will leave it or change it except on the order or with the consent of the school inspector." Things must be so arranged that "those whose parents are neglectful and verminous must be separated from those who are careful and clean; that an unruly and frivolous pupil should be placed between two who are well behaved and serious, a libertine either alone or between two pious pupils"'.*
> (Jean-Baptiste de La Salle 1783, cited in Foucault 1977: 147)

Through ordering pupils in space, they could be classified, observed, supervised and regularized with relative economy and effectiveness. In respect of this specific contemporary study of school exclusion, de La Salle's system of ordering clearly applied to the pupil Nancy who, on one occasion, had been placed in isolation daily for three weeks:

'Isolation, it's where you're in a room on your own, and you get set work from all the teachers and you're not allowed to look out, and your not allowed out. There's a toilet in the room, and they bring dinner to me.' (Nancy, see Chapter 3)

Isolation was also part of the disciplinary regime at one respondent's school as Mr DR, an in-school support worker, explained:

'The only time I'm involved in the school discipline system/sanction system is when the pupil is going to "timeout" - which is basically isolation [for two hours]. Erm, it's a sanction schools use as an alternative to a fixed-term exclusion. They come down into this room and I do what we call a "reintegration package" with them ... The idea being that you're offering some supportive measures to help them back into the classroom the following Monday ... A kid will sit behind the desk facing the front, work will be supplied, a senior member of staff will sit at the front and observe and give the kids no room to manoeuvre. They work solid. If they don't work solid, erm, they're observed and that is recorded and, unless they are 100 per cent compliant, then timeout might be extended, they might be sent home and ... we will use the fixed-term exclusion which we would have done had we not decided to give them this option.' (Mr DR, see Chapter 6)

Foucault also showed how the introduction of strict timetables in the eighteenth century allowed the behaviour of pupils to be governed in minute detail.

'"At the last stroke of the hour, a pupil will ring the bell, and at the first sound of the bell all the pupils will kneel, with their arms crossed and their eyes lowered. When the prayer has been said, the teacher will strike the signal once to indicate that the pupils should get up, a second time as a sign that they should salute Christ, and a third that they should sit down"'. (Jean-Baptiste de La Salle 1783, cited in Foucault 1977: 147)

During the interview with Mr AS, an in-school support worker, a response was interrupted by the sound of the school bell ringing. This prompted Mr AS to remark: *'you get that too, don't you? Another automatic response expected. The bells!'* (Mr AS, see Chapter 6).

In the 1840s, St Marylebone, one of London's 'Local Act' parishes, operated the following timetable in its workhouse school for children aged between 7 and 16 years:

	Boys' School		**Girls' School**
6.00-7.00	Rise, make beds, prayers, clean shoes and wash.	6.00-8.00	Rise, make beds, prayers, clean shoes, wash. Prayers and religious instruction.
7.00-7.45	Gymnastics exercises (Saturdays excepted)		
7.45-9.00	Prayers. Breakfast. Play.	8.00-9.00	Breakfast. Recreation.
9.00-10.00	Historical reading, with explanations.	9.00-11-30	Reading, spelling, tables, arithmetic.
10.00-11-00	General and mental arithmetic, tables, use of clock dial for learning the time of day.		
11.00-12-00	Grammar. Parsing and Dictation.	11.30-12-30	Working in copy books. Dictation.
12.00-2.00	Dinner. Recreation.	12.30-2-00	Dinner. Recreation.
2.00-3.00	Writing in copy books and arithmetic.	2.00-5.00	Needlework, knitting and domestic employment.
3.00-4.00	Reading with explanations.		
4.00-5.00	Geography, with maps.	5.00-6.00	Supper. Recreation.
6.00	Supper	6.00-8.00	Needlework, knitting and Domestic employment.
8-00	Prayers – retire to bed.	8-00	Prayers – retire to bed.

Source: Neate, A. R. (1967) *The St Marylebone Workhouse and Institution: 1730-1965*, St Marylebone Society, London, cited by Peter Higginbotham (2000) at users.ox.ac.uk/~peter/workhouse/education/html, 6 July 18.10, p.4.

By prescribing activities for each minute of the day, the timetable served to prevent behaviour considered wasteful, uneconomic and immoral.

Another important development in the eighteenth century was the imposition of what Foucault termed 'disciplinary time' on pedagogical practice. Effectively, this involved greater specializing in education and training, including timed programmes of learning sequenced in different stages and separated from the other by examinations and grading. Individuals would be classified by the way they progressed throughout each programme. For Foucault, these developments made possible *'a detailed control and a regular intervention (of differentiation, correction, punishment, elimination) in each moment of time'* (Foucault 1977: 160). Pupils who failed to achieve collectively useful aptitudes or acceptable ways of behaving at appropriate stages in time could easily be identified and thereby subjected to corrective treatment. Within the context of this contemporary study, it was one pupil's 'lack of aptitude' that led him into conflict with his school:

'Some of the work was hard and I used to get up and walk around and that, talk to my friends ... I used to ask them what they [the teachers] said ... I end up told off for asking questions and then ended up getting cheeky and I'd have to stand out the room and the head teacher would have to warn me. I'd have to go down to the office and stuff like that.'
(Jack, see Chapter 3)

It transpired that Jack had undiagnosed dyslexia. As his mother Jenny explained:

'They sent him to the centre when he was in Year 7 - a care centre - because he was behind on all his work. They found out that he was dyslexic - he needed extra help but he wasn't getting it at school ... Jack is in the classroom. They're all there. They're told to do a piece of work. He (the teacher) explains it and if Jack asks for it to be explained a second time he says "oh, you didn't listen the first time so just get on with it". So, if a child can't do something, there's no point in sitting there trying 'cos he can't do it. There's no use saying "you've got to sit there" when he can't do it. That's why he messes about in the classroom, 'cos they didn't give him the help he needed.'
(Jenny, see Chapter 4)

For Foucault, disciplinary practice in schools aims to maximise the contribution of individuals to a collective project - effectively, *'composing forces in order to obtain an efficient machine ... The body is constituted as part of a multi-segmentary machine'* (Foucault 1977: 164). Schools became machines for learning within which pupils, if correctly organized, would achieve the optimum results. Moreover:

'This carefully measured combination of forces requires a precise system of command. All the activity of the disciplined individual must be punctuated and sustained by injunctions whose efficacy rests on brevity and clarity; the order does not need to be explained or formulated; it must trigger off the required behaviour and that is enough. From the master of discipline to him who is subjected to it the relation is one of signalization: it is a question not of understanding the injunction but of perceiving the signal and reacting to it immediately, according to a more or less artificial, prearranged code.'
(Foucault 1977: 166)

It was the view of one support worker, Ms AF, that some pupils would never adapt to school life because of *'an inability to do what mainstream school requires - which is to do as you are told'* (Ms AF, see Chapter 6). Yet none of the excluded pupils interviewed were averse to rules and regulations at school. All but one were aware of the school rules and found them on the whole to be sensible. Significantly, it was the view of one in-school support worker that the risk of exclusion was largely connected to an *ability* of a child to challenge the school:

'If we're telling the truth about wanting to include the most challenging pupils we need to look at what we do about organising secondary schools in the future. The children who challenge because their behaviour doesn't fit the pattern, many are doing it because there are things wrong with the pattern. They are more able to reject, or not toe the line or take the standard route, and accept "this is the way you've got to be". Yes, some are disruptive. But some are the most intellectually challenging of the system and we should listen to what they're saying.' (Mr AS, see Chapter 6)

Mr TH, another in-school support worker, shared a similar position. *'Some of these youngsters are voicing what the silent majority are not always capable of saying'* (Mr TH, see Chapter 6). And yet, as this research has showed, children are not allowed to be critical of the school system, or to be involved in the process of managing their own learning or behaviour. They are not expected to have a 'voice'. As Nancy commented:

'Well, you say something to the teachers and they say "you're only 14, I'm not speaking to you". But when I was speaking to them and they are talking, it doesn't make any difference. They say to "respect your elders", but they don't give us respect. So why should we give them respect if they don't listen to you. And the other point was they all want to put you down and that. And they're butting in when I'm speaking. I get angry with it really. I just want to make them listen, and I used to shout at them and then just walk off. They just wind me up.' (Nancy, see Chapter 3)

Pamjit, an 11 year-old child attending one of the in-school support services involved in this research, captures the sense of being silenced so eloquently in the following poem:

The Cry of A Child
by Pamjit, Aged 11
Listen! Listen to the voice ...
The voice of the child that all but stilled.
No laughing or playing just crying ...
Just the crying! Crying, and the sounds of little ones dying.
Even though I'm so very small, can't you hear my voice at all?
I mind the cry of my mouth will never come to a bawl.
You ask from which country do I come?
Is it that important where I am from?
Mine, the voice of that child, wait and watch until I die!
Do see my plight
The plight of a child

This piece of poetry reflects the emotional world and needs of a child that suffers an education system that continues to adopt disciplinary practices first introduced in the eighteenth century. Those subordinated to the disciplinary regime of schooling were, and continue to be, regulated in space and time, socialised in an 'education machine' that rewards receptivity and conformity. In effect, schooling continues to reflect a 'military dream of society':

> *'Its fundamental reference was not to the state of nature, but to the meticulously subordinated cogs of a machine, not to the primal social contract, but to permanent coercions, not to fundamental rights, but to indefinitely progressive forms of training, not to the general will but to automatic docility.'* (Foucault 1977: 169)

Today, it is the national curriculum that allows central government control over the learning attributes, knowledge and skills that the central state perceive collectively useful. A corollary of this is the regulation of the teaching of these attributes at the four key stages - 7, 11, 14 and 16 years of age - and, since the Education (Schools) Act 1992, the publication of league tables. By regulating standards in this way, failing pupils and schools can be identified and treated. During New Labour's first four years of government this inspection regime for education was enhanced and extended. A new Standards and Effectiveness Unit was announced, while the government's first White Paper *Excellence in Schools* proposed targets for improvements in performance alongside new targets for literacy and numeracy. The School Standards and Framework Act 1998 gives schools two years to improve following a failed OFSTED inspection. Those that fail to improve sufficiently can be taken over and reopened as a 'Fresh Start' school (Kendall and Holloway 2001). As Anthony has argued, these regulations shape schools to become little more than feudalistic systems of control:

> *'School is a classic hierarchy: it compels attendance and obedience, and attempts to compel loyalty; it exerts discipline by means of reward and punishment; it frequently allows - or, more often, compels - those within its walls to wear special clothing proclaiming their status; and it arranges its ranks and the transmission of power in the classic feudal pyramid (principal, deputies, senior staff, senior pupils, junior pupils). All this is held somehow to be effective training for the democratic way of life, but in fact impresses the opposite social principle - hierarchy - on the youthful mind.'* (Anthony 1995: 132)

A further mechanism for controlling young minds is the school building itself. From the eighteenth century onwards the model of the military camp - designed to give maximum visibility over armed men - was increasingly applied to other forms of urban development including *'working-class housing estates, hospitals, asylums, prisons, schools'* (Foucault 1977: 171). The principle of this architectural solution is vividly portrayed in Bentham's 'panopticon', a building design comprising cells into which individuals can be confined and supervised.

The major effect of the panopticon is to *'induce in the inmate a state of conscious and permanent visibility that assures the automatic functioning of power'* (Foucault 1977: 201). The panopticon serves as an:

> *'analytical arrangement of space ... among school-children, it makes it possible to observe performances ... to map aptitudes, to assess characters, to draw up rigorous classifications and, in relation to normal development, to distinguish "laziness and stubbornness" from "incurable imbecility"'.*
> (Foucault 1977: 203)

The design and layout of school classrooms - with internal windows on corridor walls, desks laid out in rows and teachers supervising from the front - imposes on pupils a visibility aimed at ensuring their compliance. In addition, the panopticon also had an experimental function:

> *'The Panopticon was also a laboratory; it could be used as a machine to carry out experiments, to alter behaviour, to train or correct individuals ... To try out pedagogical experiments - and in particular to take up once again the well-debated problem of secluded education.'*
> (Foucault 1977: 203-204)

Bentham believed that he had devised a great new instrument of disciplinary control – *'all by a simple idea in architecture!'* (Bentham cited in Foucault 1977: 207). As Foucault asked, *'Is it surprising that prisons resemble factories, schools, barracks, hospitals, which all resemble prisons?'* (Foucault 1977: 228)

The panopticon not only served to discipline its inmates, it also provided a mechanism for supervising the supervisors. Within Bentham's design was a central tower from where the inspector could observe the occupants of each cell through its internal window. Moreover:

> *'In this central tower, the director may spy on all the employees that he has under his orders: nurses, doctors, foremen, teachers, warders; he will be able to judge them continuously, alter their behaviour, impose upon them the methods he thinks best; and it will even be possible to observe the director himself. An inspector arriving unexpectedly at the centre of the Panopticon will be able to judge at a glance, without anything being concealed from him, how the entire establishment is functioning.'*
> (Foucault 1977: 204)

In respect of schools, therefore, Bentham believed that he had devised an architectural plan capable of both exerting discipline over pupils, and regulating teachers and heads employed to exercise control. For Foucault, in time, such disciplinary practices were to become subtler than those performed by a mere model of architecture, manifesting themselves more generally *'throughout the social body'* (Foucault 1977: 207), exercised through a network of various 'discourses' and procedures seeking to normalize subjects. The disciplines of the human sciences - psychology, psychiatry, social administration, law, criminology, medicine, education and so forth - have laid claim to 'knowledge' formations that specify and distinguish 'normality' from 'abnormality':

> '*The judges of normality are present everywhere. We are in the society of the teacher-judge, the doctor-judge, the educator-judge, the "social worker" judge; it is on them that the universal reign of the normative is based.*'
> (Foucault 1977: 304)

In recent times the widespread use of school performance criteria has operated with the means of imposing a disciplinary system of judgement over teachers, enforced through the discourse of standards and quality assessment (Ball 1998). It has served to objectify the 'enemy within' the education system – 'unsatisfactory' or 'subversive' teachers and 'failing' schools. Performance indicators place teachers and schools within a system of individualising self-scrutiny. They:

> ' *"fabricate" an organisation ... for external consumption; they provide a focus for the gaze of quality and accountability; they are there to be viewed and evaluated and compared.*' (Ball 1998: 196).

Pupils, parents, teachers and support workers alike single out the dominance of the 'managerialist' discourse in education as the most destructive element within the British schooling system. What the pupil Glen most wanted to change about schools was:

> '*The way teachers teach. What they teach [the curriculum] and the number of lessons. Lessons should be more fun and interesting.*'
> (Glen, see Chapter 3)

Jim, a parent, observed:

> '*There's certainly a lot of pressure on schools today to perform, and maybe that is negative pressure, if you like, on their relationship with the pupils. There is a pressure to perform with the league tables and pressures to perform financially. Those two alone mean schools maybe haven't got enough time for the problem children. They concentrate on getting them out of the way – "let's get the good ones in, 'cos it will boost our school at the end of the year"*'. (Jim, see Chapter 4)

Mr PH, a teacher, believed that the national curriculum had the effect of turning a child into a '*commodity ... stuffed and packaged and set out into the world ... instead of looking at the child from the child's needs*' (Mr PH, see Chapter 5). Consequently, he argued that:

> '*The concept of "inclusion" is a contradiction in terms. If you are saying that everyone should be in a mainstream school, then everyone should be*

included in an environment that is right for them. If the education system was set up to meet everyone's needs then all pupils would be in the right place of learning. Instead, all pupils have to meet set standards which, for some, may not be meaningful.' (Mr PH, see Chapter 5)

Mr RR, another teacher, also saw the regulatory framework for education as problematic:

'At the end of the day you are results driven - we are pushing, pushing, pushing for the improvement of exam results. And we get the improvement of exam results, but penalise the certain pupils who don't fit in easily with the system.' (Mr RR, see Chapter 5)

He thought that teachers particularly lacked time:

'We don't have the time to sit for hours and talk to children who need our help because we are under pressure to improve our assessment and exam results, or to complete our performance pay application form. They reward teachers who have demonstrated the ability to write something coherent on eight pages of an application form ... They don't see the relationship teachers have with the kids. The pieces of paper I have had to fill in so that somebody else can judge if I'm worthy of my salary! It's getting a bit out of hand!'
(Mr RR, see Chapter 5)

Support workers shared similar concerns about the role of the regulation of schools in nourishing exclusions. Mr MB, for instance, argued that:

'It is a mess. If I were to blame anybody, or look to see what's gone wrong, things like league tables haven't helped schools. Schools are aware that these will be published; they are aware that people will be looking at the percentage of A to Cs. If they've got students who are poor attenders or who disrupt the class they're not going to be sympathetic to that student. They are going to want that student out.' (Mr MB, see Chapter 6)

Similarly, Mr DR, also a support worker, believed that there was insufficient time for schools to give to:

'the social development of the child ... [and that] ... you've got to point the finger at the government for having set up such massive bureaucratic systems ... which teachers are far too preoccupied with.'
(Mr DR, see chapter 6)

Ms DB, another support worker, also believed that the education system was placing undue pressures on teachers that, in turn, impacted detrimentally on the well-being of *all* pupils:

'I think that there is a lot, erm, of new initiatives in the last few years. I think teachers are under enormous pressure to deliver the national curriculum, performance management, and all these targets. And that comes from the top down. And that pressure is transferred from the senior management to the teachers, and the teachers transfer that pressure to the pupils. The pupils haven't got anywhere to put that pressure.'
(Ms DB, see Chapter 6)

Ms MH, head of a behavioural support centre, supported this position:

'If we could get away from that competitiveness mentality to say that every single child is a wanted child ... We concentrate on the wrong things really. If we could concentrate on the difficult children, and make them feel welcome and part of the school ... And every other child is going to benefit from that by the positive way in which you treat them.'
(Ms MH, see Chapter 6)

Instruments of control in education are not solely about regulating the 'recalcitrant' pupil or 'ineffective' teacher. They also extend to the judgement and disciplining of parents and carers, a continuation of what Foucault saw as the 'swarming of disciplinary mechanisms':

'Thus the Christian School must not simply train docile children; it must also make it possible to supervise the parents, to gain information as to their way of life, their resources, their piety, their morals. The school tends to constitute minute social observatories that penetrate even to the adults and exercise regular supervision over them: the bad behaviour of the child, or his absence, is a legitimate pretext ... for one to go and question the neighbours, especially if there is any reason to believe the family will not tell the truth; one can then go and question the parents themselves, to find out whether they know their catechism and the prayers, whether they are determined to root out the vices of their children, how many beds there are in the house and what the sleeping arrangements are.'
(Foucault 1977: 211)

In the name of tackling 'social exclusion' and anti-social behaviour New Labour have introduced 'truancy sweeps', heavy fines, plans to withhold benefits and the threat of court action against parents and carers of pupils out of school. All in all, these measures appear to conform neatly to Foucault's thesis, combining to produce an overarching strategy aimed at ensuring the docility of pupils, teachers, and parents and carers. The effect is an education system that suffocates prospects for more liberating, innovative, dialogical pedagogical processes, tolerant of difference and diversity. Moreover, as Michael Young suggests, it is a system that perpetuates dominant power relationships in society:

'Ability of a conventional kind ... has become much more highly

concentrated by the engine of education. A social revolution has been accomplished by harnessing schools and universities to the task of sieving people according to education's narrow band of values. With an amazing battery of certificates and degrees at its disposal, education has put its seal of approval on a minority, and its seal of disapproval on the many who fail to shine from the time they are relegated to the bottom streams at the age of seven or before. The new class has the means at hand, and largely under its control, by which it reproduces itself.' (Young 2001: 17)

Alongside similar policies targeting rough sleepers, truants, pregnant teenagers and deprived housing estates, New Labour's approach to education is part of a broader scheme:

'... about the pursuit of moral conformity and social order, presented as help ... Those who fail to fall in line with the dominant morality are stigmatised.' (Levitas 2001: 2)

It is within this wider context that the refusal of young minds to comply with the established norms of the education system can be more clearly understood. As this piece of contemporary research has shown, it is also a context within which teachers, support workers and parents (and arguably all of us) are dominated and regulated. Given this, it is not too unrealistic to predict, as Tomlinson argues, a reaction against the *'centrally imposed curriculum, the unfairness of inspection and assessment, control of educational institutions, contempt for local democratic input, and the narrow economic concept of education which dominated by 2000'* (Tomlinson 2001: 171). The key task in education, therefore, is to build a new alliance - comprising teachers, unions, parents' associations, community youth workers and other interested parties, to work together to expose and challenge the inherent contradictions in New Labour's welfare discourse. We need to reclaim education as a:

'humanizing, liberalizing, democratizing force, directed, as the UN (1948) Universal Declaration of Human Rights put it, to "the full development of the human personality and a strengthening of respect for human rights and fundamental freedoms"'. (Tomlinson 2001: 171)

Through reforming our education system in this way, we may possibly start to build a more inclusive society in the future.

Summary and conclusion

Throughout its history, the state education system appears to have retained a role that has significant value for sustaining dominant power relationships in society. As a consequence, pupils who challenge this disciplinary regime are victimised by its strict practices. At the same time, teachers are increasingly colonised within the system, stripped of their 'professionalism' and enforced to implement the state's bidding - the transmission of a highly prescriptive and largely questionable curriculum. Respondents to this research raise significant concerns about the value of this curriculum and how it is taught. These concerns suggest that social inclusion through education in Britain, a policy New Labour is committed to, is not possible until the system itself adopts different pedagogical values that respect the learning needs of a diverse range of pupils. Such a shift would allow all pupils to be valued and allow space for children to develop their learning around their own enthusiasms. It would also see teachers appreciated in different ways, such as their ability to relate and empathise with children and young people - in contrast to today's narrow obsession with dubious criteria of success. Consideration also needs to be given to the broader context in which children and young people live their lives in Britain - including support for families and genuine attention to poverty issues, difficult neighbourhood circumstances and unpromising futures.

References

Anthony, E. (1995) *Thy Rod and Staff*, London: Little, Brown and Company.

Ball, S.J. (1998) 'Performativity and fragmentation in postmodern schooling', in Carter, J. (ed), *postmodernity and the fragmentation of welfare*, London: Routledge, pp. 187-203.

Foucault, M. (1977) *Discipline and Punish: The Birth of the Prison*, Harmondsworth: Penguin.

Kendall, I. and Holloway, D. (2001) 'Education Policy' in Savage, S.P. and Atkinson, R. (eds.), *Public Policy Under Blair*, Basingstoke: Palgrave, pp.154-173.

Levitas, R. (2001) 'Government more concerned with conformity than poverty', *Guardian Society*, 23 March, society.guardian.co.uk/socialexclusion/story/0,11499,630786,00.html, 18/1/02, pp.1-3

Tomlinson, S. (2001) *Education in a post-welfare society*, Buckingham: Open University Press.

Usher, R. and Edwards, R. (1994) *Postmodernism and Education*, London: Routledge.

Young, M. (2001) 'Down with meritocracy', *The Guardian*, 29 June, p.17.